D1136962

A FREE COUNTRY?

John Tanburn

Book Guild Publishing

Sussex, England

First published in Great Britain in 2015 by
The Book Guild Ltd
The Werks
45 Church Road
Hove, BN3 2BE

Copyright © John Tanburn 2015

The right of John Tanburn to be identified as the author of
this work has been asserted by him in accordance with the
Copyright, Designs and Patents Act 1988.

All rights reserved. No part of this publication may be reproduced, transmitted, or stored
in a retrieval system, in any form or by any means, without permission in writing from
the publisher, nor be otherwise circulated in any form of binding or cover other than
that in which it is published and without a similar condition being imposed on the
subsequent purchaser.

Haringey Libraries	
TT	
Askews & Holts	25-May-2015
323.44	
	HAOL22/4/15

Typesetting in Garamond by
YHT Ltd, London

Printed and bound in Great Britain by
CPI Group (UK) Ltd, Croydon, CR0 4YY

A catalogue record for this book is available from
The British Library

ISBN 978 1 910508 02 2

For
Richard and Lucas

Contents

Acknowledgements

I thank Professor Matthew Kramer, Professor of Legal and Political Philosophy at Cambridge University, for allowing me to attend his lectures on jurisprudence, which have helped me to sharpen up some of the thinking in chapter 2, to my wife Renée for patiently ploughing through successive drafts of chapter 5 and making helpful suggestions, and to my son James for his very thoughtful and distinctive comments. He is an authority on outcome measurement in development, and his help has been invaluable, especially in chapter 14.

Introduction

[Freedom] is ... the indispensable condition for the quest for human completion.
Paolo Freire

A long time ago, I took a degree in law at Cambridge. One of the options in the last year of the course was jurisprudence, which is the philosophy of law. It was the only part of the course which really interested me. I was not going into the legal profession, and I devoted many of my hours to other pursuits, so I did not get a particularly good degree. By sheer chance, some 43 years later, I met my old tutor, by then Professor R.Y. Jennings and a judge at the International Court of Justice at The Hague. I was amazed that he remembered me, and even more so when he told me that I had been 'top man' in my year in jurisprudence. I am neither an academic nor a lawyer. Apart from creating law departments in two schools and teaching the subject to what was then O level, I have had no further professional contact with the law, but I have never lost a passion for freedom and an interest in jurisprudence.

Just how precious is our freedom? The number of choices available to us determines how fully we can develop our human potential. John Stuart Mill conclusively showed in his classic *On Liberty* that freedom is not just a juridical concept, but is essential to our well-being. Freedom is also essential to innovation, creativity and diversity in science and in the arts, in universities' research and teaching, in industry and in commerce. It is essential to the growth and health of both human beings and the economy, of both our personal and our social lives.

Like our health, it is often only when we have lost it that we realise just how vital it is. Short of capital punishment, depriving people of their freedom is the most severe punishment in the Western world. Imprisonment has a particular horror, both for those who have experienced it and for those who have not, except for those most institutionalised. In prison, the finest degrees of freedom become important in the form of privileges. Lesser forms of deprivation of freedom, such as disqualification from driving, also have severe consequences and are much feared. The law has also always taken a very serious view of wrongful imprisonment. For centuries, ever since Magna Carta in 1215, British courts have treated the freedom of the individual citizen as a supreme value, and its protection as one of their main functions. In the past, one of their prime instruments for protecting the individual's freedom was the writ of habeas corpus, by which they would summon anyone detaining another to produce the detained person in court and account for the detention. A hearing on a writ of habeas corpus took precedence over all other court business. Now, habeas corpus is rarely used. We shall look further at this issue in Chapter 5.

Despite this precious tradition, it seems that our freedom is in danger as never before. The old dangers of officious and intrusive government are always there. Continuing technological advances hugely leverage up the old threats and also create entirely new ones. The threat does not come now from a single foreign country: it is more complicated and insidious.

This work is an ambitious attempt to sketch the profile of a truly free country against which to measure our own; a jurisprudence for freedom. There is in jurisprudence a large literature on competing theories of freedom and of rights, and methods of measuring the freedom of an individual. Jurisprudents will recognise the ghost of Hohfeld wandering through Chapter 2, now haunting not the world of persons but of the state, and translated into the language of everyday life; that of the constitutional jurist A.V. Dicey in Chapter 5, and the spirit of John Stuart Mill throughout. But jurisprudents live in academia, and we badly need them to get out into the social and political marketplace and provide the intellectual groundwork for freedom in our own time. Not being an academic is my qualification for addressing this work primarily to people without a background in law. I have tried to avoid jargon, and to keep the work short and accessible. I have kept Chapters 7–16 very short for this reason, so I run the risk of being accused of over-simplification: I accept responsibility for that. I have also decided against a bibliography because all references can easily be found on the web. I particularly recommend the Online Library of Liberty (oll.libertyfund.org, hereinafter OLL), where all the key texts and much more can be found. Other sources I have embedded in the text.

In addition, I have drawn on *The Assault on Liberty* by Dominic Raab (Fourth Estate, 2009, hereinafter, Raab). Mr Raab, who has a distinguished legal background, accumulated a mass of useful facts to support his thesis that an unprecedented assault on our liberty was being launched. This is still an invaluable resource, even though much more could now be added. If I have one regret about the book, it is that Mr Raab, a Conservative MP writing in the dying days of the Gordon Brown administration, blames Labour for all assaults on liberty. This is surely far too important to be made into a party matter. It is a constitutional issue, even a human one, and is rightly the concern of a cross-party parliamentary group. I myself am not a member of any political party, and I would like this work to be seen as independent of party politics.

I wonder, too, what view Mr Raab takes of the record of the Conservative-led coalition in rolling back all the excessive legislation of the Blair and Brown years. The Protection of Freedoms Act 2012 has been a long time in gestation and does not seem to have been a priority in the legislative programme. If it leads to real changes in its specific areas, that is a step in the right direction, but a modern Magna Carta it is not.

I have also drawn on *Freedom as Development* by Amartya Sen (OUP, 1999, hereinafter Sen), a wonderful exposition of the whole enterprise of development as being both accomplished and measured by the freedom secured for its beneficiaries. We shall see that, by this standard, we need to look to our own development.

Liberty is a beautiful word, but to many people it seems a remote and abstract term appearing mainly in intellectual discourse. Freedom, on the other hand, has an immediate visceral charge and is a familiar word in common use. Reluctantly, therefore, I have chosen freedom as the term for use here. Where 'liberty' occurs, it means the same as freedom. *He* and *she* are to be read as interchangeable except when referring to a named person.

We are not here concerned with personal limitations on freedom, or inabilities. Some are endowed with strong, well co-ordinated bodies, others with bodies that are defective in some way. Some have great intelligence, others less. The first group in each case has much more freedom, many more choices, than the second. Further, we all experience the frustration that arises from conflicting needs and impulses within ourselves. These limitations on our personal freedom are hugely important to us, but they are not our subject here. Here we focus on freedom under the law.

When Machiavelli wrote in *The Prince* that a prince who takes a city that has been accustomed to live in freedom must either destroy the city or be destroyed by it, he meant a city that has not been governed or taxed by another state. He is referring to state autonomy, not to the freedom of the individual citizen. State autonomy is a major issue in our times also, threatened and diminished as it is by large transnational corporations, by other transnational entities, and by the process of globalisation, threatening and undermining democracy. Important and urgent as it is, this too is not our focus here. 'A free country' in this book is a country that values and protects the freedom of the individual citizen.

Also outside the scope of this book are the ancient philosophical debates on free will and determinism, together with their modern versions such as the nature-nurture debate, and the classics on the inner liberation of the spirit. Keeping the focus firmly on the legal frameworks will provide more than enough for one book.

Chapter 1 is the hors d'oeuvres; Chapters 2 to 6 are the main course; and the rest of Section 3 is the desserts: a series of short essays in no particular order, intended as tasters rather than exhaustive treatments. Each of these subjects commands not just a book but a whole literature. I have even omitted some important freedom-related issues, such as academic freedom, in an attempt to keep the book accessibly and digestibly short. Bon appétit!

Writing this has been a race with events. Scarcely a day goes by without some new, and often dramatic, development requiring alteration to one or more chapters. This work will therefore date fast, like Raab but unlike Mill, whose *On Liberty* has not to my knowledge been out of print since it was published in 1859.

The year 2015 is the 800th anniversary of Magna Carta, and a once-in-a-lifetime opportunity to press for a modern version: one that will restore and strengthen the historic safeguards of our freedom, and address the new issues raised by the technologies of surveillance and information storage. The worst thing that could happen is a series of showpiece events, perhaps involving the Queen, full of high-flown rhetoric that changes nothing. Watch out for abstract nouns like liberty, equality, access, justice, democracy and tolerance. Abstract nouns are not enforceable at law, unlike Magna Carta 1.0, and would amount to cynical window-dressing. With the general election past, we can hope that the new House of Commons Political and Constitutional Reform Select Committee will expedite the work of its predecessor, which was considering the merits of a written constitution, and push ahead with its consultation on a new Magna Carta. We must see to it that it at least restores and strengthens the social contract first sketched in Magna Carta 1.0 and also addresses the novel issues raised by the technologies of surveillance and information storage. The committee is open to submissions. See chapters 5 and 16 for more.

2015 is also the bicentenary of the Battle of Waterloo. Our freedom is the common factor in both commemorations.

My hope is that readers of this book will be increasingly informed, vigilant and above all active in restoring, protecting and enlarging our freedom, in particular by supporting the work of the relevant campaigning organisations, of which more later.

> *The only thing necessary for the triumph of evil*
> *is for good men to do nothing.*
> Edmund Burke

Section 1
Defining 'A Free Country'

1

Defining Freedom

*The world has never had a good definition of the word 'liberty.'...
In using the same word, we do not mean the same thing.*
Abraham Lincoln

What is freedom? The Roman Empire had a highly developed
legal system. Its concept of freedom was closely linked to
that of citizenship. A Roman citizen was free: that freedom
was restricted to free-born male residents. Nowadays we
might describe that as privilege rather than freedom. Roman
law knew nothing of freedom as the birthright of all; indeed,
slavery was an essential part of the economy.

In our own times, definitions have tended to focus on
freedom *from* and freedom *to*, or 'negative' and 'positive'
freedom, but still without defining the essence of the term.
The *Oxford English Dictionary* gives more emphasis to
freedom *from*, but no definition has been comprehensive.

The basic and essential text on the subject is *On Liberty,* by
John Stuart Mill. His central statement is: '... the only purpose
for which power can be rightfully exercised over any member of a civilised community, against his will, is to prevent
harm to others'. Mill's harm principle is central to all thinking
about freedom. He makes an overwhelming case for liberty as

essential to human well-being, but he does not offer a definition. Perhaps he thought it was obvious.

Yet his work was strongly opposed when it was published in 1859. The British establishment was still terrified by the French Revolution of 1789. It had proved infectious, and as recently as 1848 there had been revolutions in several European countries. *Liberty* was too close for comfort to *Liberté, Egalité, Fraternité*, and his work was seen by some as subversive.

1.1 Freedom and anarchy

Such a reaction is not surprising if freedom is confused with anarchy. In a state of anarchy, individuals consider themselves free to do whatever they like, regardless of the consequences for others. They then discover that their neighbour's 'freedom' impinges on their own. In a state of anarchy, my neighbour considers herself free to assault me, to invade my property, to steal my goods and to destroy my reputation. The result is chaos.

Yet it is surprising how many passionate and articulate people confuse freedom with anarchy. Extreme free-marketeers (chapter 12), extreme free-speech advocates (usually in the media, with a special interest – chapter 5), extreme advocates for 'the open internet' (also chapter 5), who argue against regulation of any kind, appear to be arguing for anarchy disguised as freedom. The big beasts in the jungle naturally want no restraint on their ability to crush or exploit lesser organisms, which they see as their natural and rightful prey. They seldom pause in their passionate advocacy of 'freedom' for their own activities to offer their own distinction between freedom and anarchy.

Among those who shout for freedom are not a few
Who mean freedom for me but not for you.

To see clearly the difference, the contrast, between freedom and anarchy, we have only to look at the internet. This unprecedented experiment in human relations is still at the primal, anarchic stage. We shall look in chapter 3 at the implications for privacy; here we note that, in the online world, the law of the jungle prevails. At the global level, we are witnessing a battle for control of the territory between the big beasts, such as Google, Apple, Microsoft, Facebook, Twitter and Amazon, as the smaller beasts carve out specialist niches or perish. At the user level, 'trolls', terrorists, criminals and paedophiles can and do use the net and the 'darknet' to damage people, governments and organisations. Malicious anonymous posts, which may be untrue, can ruin our reputation, our career and our marriage, and we have little or no recourse. The most vulnerable are inevitably damaged or destroyed, particularly children. Imagine a similar scene on our streets, and you begin to see the difference between anarchy and freedom.

This is not to say that nothing good happens in an anarchic state. On the contrary, the internet has given us immeasurable new choices and possibilities. It is to say, however, that the law of the jungle prevails, and our only protection from predators is what we can provide or buy for ourselves. This is a stage of human social development that has in the past preceded civilisation.

The experiment in anarchy has only just begun. If we extrapolate from present experience, there seems to be no reason why one or more of the big companies could not come to dominate and control the entire internet. Google started with the apparently altruistic aim of making all information available to all people. Looking at the back of the tapestry, however, that could look like a bid to control all the information. All the weird, fictional dreams of world domination come to mind: control not by force but by information. Who controls all the information in the world controls the world.

This is not a far-fetched fantasy. On 28th September 2014, no less an authority than Sir Tim Berners-Lee said:

'If a company can control your access to the internet, if they can control which websites you go to, then they have tremendous control over your life,' he told the Web We Want festival. 'If a government can block you going to, for example, the opposition's political pages, then they can give you a blinkered view of reality to keep themselves in power. 'Suddenly the power to abuse the open internet has become tempting both for government and big companies.' He called for a world-wide digital Magna Carta to protect the freedom of the web user (Source: *The Telegraph*, 29/9/14).

Without naming particular companies, he added that the large information corporations would 'love to be able to take control of the internet market' and 'use it to establish control of some other markets.' (Source: *The Times*, 29/9/14)

There is real fear across Europe of the power of Google. Germany's Federal Cartel Office has produced a 30-page dossier listing in detail measures open to its government to limit the power of such bodies, for example treating them as utilities and controlling their advertising charges. This document focuses on the haemorrhage of money rather than that of information, but it shows that the two are inextricably bound together: both transfer power and therefore freedom. (Source: *The Sunday Times* business section, 13/7/14).

Meanwhile, technology advances at an exponential rate for both good and ill. National legislators cannot even hope to keep ahead of it, much less international negotiators. There is no global authority to regulate or control use of the internet, no rule of law and no prospect of any.

While governments may be alarmed at the huge outflows of money, their real interests do not lie in alienating such companies. On the contrary, governments are very glad of the information they can glean, legally or illegally, from their traffic. The interests of governments do not lie in controlling or antagonising internet companies, but in using them as sources of information about their own citizens and those of other countries. Between national governments and internet companies there is a convergence of interests, not a conflict. If government connivance with commercial companies continues when it is not needed, or more than is needed, the shepherd has then made a deal with the wolf.

Governments, for their part, believe, or start out believing, or at least claim, that they are protecting their citizens by engaging in universal covert surveillance. We shall look in chapter 6 at the question of how far this is really the case.

Freedom, as opposed to anarchy, is only possible in a country possessing a legal structure that protects the freedom of each citizen and balances the freedom of each against that of others, and against the abuse of power by the state. So freedom in a free country means freedom under the law.

1.2 Freedom and the rule of law

The internet, then, demonstrates anarchy, not freedom. What separates freedom from anarchy is the rule of law. By balancing the freedom of each individual against that of others, by protecting the individual against abuse of power, it makes every citizen responsible for her choices and actions, and their consequences. Thus individual responsibility will form part of our proposed definition of a free country in chapter 4.

However, the rule of law is not as straightforward a concept as it seems. There is such a thing as bad law. Both Hitler and Stalin operated entirely within the law. They could claim to be upholding the rule of law, and stigmatise anyone who dared to dissent, or to challenge their actions, as breaking the law and attacking the rule of law. Closer to home, there are laws that are bad in a number of ways: inconsistent, unclear or unenforceable laws are oppressive, the very antithesis of freedom. Bad laws put the otherwise law-abiding citizen in a bind: he may have conscientiously to break the law. Indeed, it has been argued that, since the rule of law means that citizens are responsible, there will be occasions when the rule of law positively *requires* active protest. It will always be a matter for the individual conscience to decide when such action is required; in a free country, it will always be put before a jury to decide whether such protest is justified and proportionate. Juries have sometimes refused to convict in such cases.

It is a different thing when individuals or classes consider themselves above the law and unaccountable, and behave accordingly. This is unprincipled, arbitrary and exploitative; it profits the individual in some way (not necessarily financial) at the expense of others. The rule of law is broken and the freedom of others impaired. At various times, the very wealthy, members of 'upper' classes, of government and of the police have behaved in this way. In chapter 5, we shall look at current examples. When any person or group behaves as if above the law, it is essential that they be punished, and be seen to be punished, if public respect for the rule of law and for freedom is to be maintained. In a free country, no one is above the law.

For our purposes, then, we ask not whether individuals are free, but whether a country is free, in the sense that the protection and enlargement of the freedom of the individual citizen is the primary function of all its legal institutions. Individual freedom depends on and flows from that. The constitutional structures essential to ensure freedom will be examined in more detail in chapter 5, with an enquiry into the state of repair of those structures today.

1.3 Freedom and freedoms

We need also to distinguish between freedom and freedoms. There are discrete, specific freedoms, such as freedoms of belief, of assembly and of speech. Discrete freedoms are not our subject here. We are looking at overall freedom, one and indivisible, the condition of a country where the freedom of the individual citizen is the value informing and shaping all its legal institutions and held by all as a primary value. (We shall distinguish freedoms from rights in chapter 2.)

1.4 Freedom and independence

We also distinguish freedom from independence. We are dependent on each other in countless ways. Independence, or self-sufficiency, is largely a fantasy. It is a fantasy that is important to us, especially when we grow up, move out of our parents' home, earn our first wage and become self-supporting. Our independence is something to celebrate! But we soon discover that we are dependent on many others: employers, colleagues and friends; on banks and lenders; on public utilities and services such as police and transport. It is even more fundamental than that: all organisms live by trading, that is, by taking some substances in from the environment and putting others out. This holds true right down to the level of the individual cell. Our dependence on each other makes us vulnerable to each other. In a free country, the law exists to protect and balance our vulnerabilities, not to make us independent. Only when the law does this efficiently can we be free.

Similarly, in relationships where the power is unevenly distributed so that one party is dependent on the other, as between employers and employees or between landlords and tenants, the law has often had to step in to protect the

15

dependent party against ruthless exploitation. A country is only as free as its least free citizens.

1.5 So what is freedom?

Even when we have distinguished freedom from anarchy, from freedoms and from independence, we are still short of a definition of freedom. Thomas Hobbes, the English political philosopher (d. 1679) offered this definition in *Of Liberty and Necessity*: 'Liberty is the absence of all the impediments to action that are not contained in the nature and intrinsical quality of the agent.'

These 'impediments' are anything experienced as such, not just repressive laws. Mill, living in middle-class, mid-Victorian London, found that informal social pressures to conformity were a much more potent constraint on freedom than oppressive legislation.

A variant form of 'negative' liberty is the 'republican' version: freedom is not the absence of impediments but the absence of domination. You are free if there is no one to whom you have to defer. This relates only to social structures, and does not seem to account for Mill's informal pressures, contemporary versions of which we shall look at briefly in chapter 2, section 2.1.2. Philip Pettit's book *Just Freedom* (W.W. Norton & Co. Ltd., 2014) is a recent and lucid advocacy of the republican view.

These are versions of the currently accepted view, that of 'negative liberty'. Rousseau carried the negative view to its logical conclusion in his *Social Contract* of 1762: he was writing in the run-up to the French Revolution of 1789. The state represents 'the will of the people', and freedom is merely what is left over after the citizen has discharged his duties to the state, which the state alone defines. This led to a horrifying dictatorship of the majority. We shall argue later in

16

this work for constitutional safeguards against that outcome in a modern Magna Carta.

This essentially negative view sees freedom as an absence rather than as a presence. It is rather like defining peace as the absence of conflict or health as the absence of disease. It seems not so much wrong as inadequate. We want a more positive view, to see freedom as a presence, rather as we see a very healthy and vigorous person, such as a successful athlete, footballer or mountaineer, not as one who escapes disease, but as someone who enjoys a positive condition.

Such a positive view seems to be implied by the ancient concept of The King's Peace, and hence a Justice of the Peace and a Breach of the Peace. The King's Peace is Magna Carta's expression of the view that the state exists to maintain order, and the purpose of that order is to protect the freedom of the individual citizen. We cannot make a breach in an absence: the peace, with the freedom it protects, is a positive condition. The concept of a breach of the peace has been taken up in modern times by the Charter of the United Nations, particularly in Chapter VII on the role of the Security Council.

Unfashionable as it might be, we could choose to stand Hobbes's definition (or Pettit's) on its head and see impediments or constraint (or domination) as the absence of freedom, not the other way round. If we have forgotten what a positively free country would look like, that would show clearly how far from it we already are, how comfortably institutionalised we have already become.

In our quest for a working definition of a free country, we now turn in chapter 2 to its relation to human rights and to rights in general. Are they the same thing as freedom, or something different? When we have explored that topical issue, we encounter in chapter 3 one even more controversial and complex: the relationship, if any, between freedom and privacy. We shall then be in a better position to suggest in chapter 4 a definition of a free country for our own technological times, so different from Mill's.

> *The price of freedom is constant vigilance.*
> Variously attributed

2

Freedom and Human Rights

*We hold these truths to be self-evident, that all men are created
equal, that they are endowed by their Creator with certain
unalienable Rights, that among these are Life, Liberty and the
pursuit of Happiness.*
The American Declaration of Independence

We shall distinguish in this chapter between human rights
and rights in general: we shall severely question the notion
that all human beings have rights simply by virtue of being
human, but strongly support *citizen* rights as legislated
within states on a constitutional basis of freedom.

Human rights arouse hot passions. Some feel strongly that
when people are deprived of (what they consider to be) basic
rights, this diminishes their very humanity and is intolerable
wherever it happens. At the opposite extreme, there are
regimes and individuals to whom the concept makes no
sense whatever. It is simply an obstacle to progress, and the
upholders of rights are interfering and subversive hypocrites.
Between these extremes, there are more selective and
nuanced views that are, nevertheless, held with equal passion. Even to question human rights might seem like questioning motherhood. Yet the very concept needs scrutiny and

testing against reality. Three objections have been raised by several thinkers and writers.

2.1 Three objections to *human* rights

2.1.1 Are there any such things as human rights?

Human rights are a major political issue, but not a new one. A key word in the quotation that opens this chapter is *all*. Are there really moral norms, such as rights, that apply to all people in all countries at all times, solely by virtue of being human? The idea of a universal moral code goes back to Aristotle, and has been developed since in different forms and often described as 'natural law'. In religious cultures and periods, such norms are seen as having divine authority, as with Thomas Aquinas, the mediaeval scholar. In more humanist or secular societies, other grounds for natural law have been sought, notably by Grotius, the seventeenth-century philosopher. The moral authority of natural law has fluctuated, the content has varied, and it has remained largely unwritten and unenforceable.

In our own times, we prefer a scientific discourse. We might seek a basis for universal norms, or natural law, in the simple fact that we are a gregarious species. We do not live solitary lives, like polar bears or foxes. The true loner among us is rare, and is always regarded with intense suspicion. We live together in settlements such as villages and towns. It then becomes obvious that the services required, such as defence, law and order, roads, schools and clinics, can only be provided communally, all individuals contributing to a common fund to achieve common ends. This will give rise to an increasingly complex web of mutual rights and duties. We form communities, and we call this civilisation. If there are such things as universal norms, therefore, they will consist of requiring behaviours that are conducive to the unity, security and health of the community, and forbidding behaviours that have negative social consequences. The exigencies of communal living can be seen as the basis of any morality or law that might exist across times and cultures.

Does this give rise to rights that can be called *human* rights because they are *necessarily* implied by the social living that is characteristic of our species? Is it true that we have certain rights simply by virtue of being human?

Arguably, the individual might claim a right to be protected by the community from external threats in return for his loyalty and participation, because if the community abandons its members when threatened it cannot expect their whole-hearted commitment.

Yet even this right is not absolute. In some circumstances, the community will instead eject the threatened member, for example when the individual becomes a threat. Historically, the exclusion of lepers is the obvious example. In extreme famine, such as in a besieged city, the community cannot support those who cannot support themselves, so widows and the disabled may be excluded. In a society where a dowry is required for a girl to be married, girl babies may be abandoned because this later liability could cripple the family.

Even the definition of a threat that merits protection will vary from culture to culture. Does sickness give the right to communal treatment if the sick person or their family cannot afford it? This is a very hot issue in the USA at present. Each country makes its own decision, so even the right to community protection is culturally variable, and therefore not a universal or 'human' right.

Different rights and freedoms (see chapter 1) are given to different groups in different countries. Women, married couples, children, slaves, foreigners, captives, criminals, the insane, royalty, nobility and legislators may be given (or take) different statuses, freedoms and rights in different cultures, or

21

in the same culture at different times. Even other species may have a special status in some cultures, such as cows for Hindus or cats in ancient Egypt.

Rights and freedoms, therefore, are not universal norms. We are not born with freedoms or rights in our genes. We do not have them just by being human. They are conferred by governments and can be attenuated or withdrawn by governments. So there are no *human* rights, nor are all people born free. There are all too many people born into the world without either.

Despite that hard reality, a kind of wistful longing for universal rights has lingered through the centuries, surfacing occasionally in the writings of philosophers. Thomas Paine was the first to set out a system of rights in *The Rights of Man* (1791-92). He was influential in framing the American Declaration of Independence and the Constitution, and the Constitution adopted by the French National Assembly after the Revolution of 1789. However, the excesses that followed the French Revolution disillusioned him, and the revolutions that followed throughout the nineteenth century tended to discredit ideas of equality, rights and even freedom.

Adam Smith wrote of 'rights [that] belong to a man as a man', stating, almost as an echo of Magna Carta (see section 2.2.1 in this chapter), that 'the first and chief design of all civill [sic] government is ... to maintain each individual in his perfect rights' (Introduction to Lectures on Jurisprudence, 1762-63). He goes on to analyse these rights as a man's rights not to be damaged in his person, his reputation or his estate. These are rights against all others, not against specific persons or bodies; they are rights not to be hindered or damaged, and so might today be described as freedoms rather than as rights. As Professor of Philosophy at Glasgow University, Smith was teaching within a framework where the rule of law and a basis of freedom were established,

22

understood and experienced, by his students. It was a mere preamble to his lectures, establishing common ground.

The concept resurfaced in 1948 when the General Assembly of the United Nations agreed the Universal Declaration of Human Rights (UDHR), followed by several conventions featuring particular vulnerable groups. The United Nations chose to construct human rights as a universal, absolute truth. The first clause of the UDHR begins: 'All human beings are born free and equal in dignity and rights.' Article 3 reads: 'Everyone has the right to life, liberty and security of person.' The term 'rights' is used as a universal norm, a moral absolute, not as culturally relative. Similarly, Article 2 contains the words: 'No distinction shall be made on the basis of the political, jurisdictional or international status of the country or territory to which a person belongs, whether it be independent, trust, non-self-governing or under any other limitation of sovereignty.'

The UDHR, then, asserts that these rights are universal, not culturally relative. Thus the paradox is that, although rights vary from country to country, one group of countries committed itself to the view that *all* people have (not *should* have) certain rights, described as human rights, even the citizens of non-signatory states. This purports to impose on the governments of those states an equivalent duty to respect and protect such rights. This has the effect, and was intended to have the effect, of polarising all countries that do not sign up to the Declaration, of putting them 'in the wrong'.

This was a natural reaction at the time. It was only in 1945 that the atrocities of the Nazi concentration camps were revealed. Newsreels showed the footage shot by American soldiers from their jeeps as they rolled into Bergen-Belsen, with rows of living skeletons in indescribable filth and squalor. As the scale of the Holocaust became clear, with about six million people systematically degraded and murdered in a whole system of concentration camps, the world's shock and revulsion led to the determination that nothing like it should ever happen again. Together with the horror of two world wars in a generation, moral absolutes seemed called for. The British were among the nations most strongly advocating and framing the UDHR.

Since 1948, the concept of human rights has been developed in many directions. The European Court of Human Rights has steadily expanded the scope of the European Convention on Human Rights (ECHR), enlarging its role by inventing new rights that are then binding on member states.

We have seen that the reality is that there are no such things as human rights. The statements of the UDHR and other conventions on human rights (including the ECHR) are really ideals or aspirations, not facts. We shall see that stating ideals as facts has consequences.

Is freedom different in this respect? As with rights, people in different cultures are born with varying degrees of freedom. Until the American Civil War in the 1860s, some people there were born slaves, despite the earlier declaration at the head of this chapter. Freedom is as culturally varied and relative as rights, but the USA chose to construct it, in the Declaration of Independence, as a universal, absolute truth, just as the United Nations was later to do with 'human' rights.

We have only to look at these absolutes created by the UDHR and the USA from a point of view in the East to see how relative they are. In many parts of the world with cultures and traditions different from those of the West, both freedom and rights are seen as alien concepts. The idea of freedom may make little sense in a theocracy such as a Muslim state; equality none at all in a Hindu caste structure. Constructing human rights or freedom as universal moral absolutes risks the United Nations being seen as an instrument of Western powers, and any attempt to introduce freedom, equality or democracy into other cultures as a particularly hypocritical form of imperialism, its agents as the

24

new secular missionaries. (Any attempt to impose freedom by force is also laughably contradictory.)

It is not just Western powers that construct such universal absolutes. Muslims believe in one god, the creator of the universe and the judge of all people. For Muslims, it is a duty to bring all people to submission to god and his law, the *sharia*, seen as an universal moral absolute.

At least the United Nations attempted universality by inviting all nations to sign up. The absurdity of the position becomes more focused with the creation of the ECHR. How could rights be both European and universal? Such rights are unenforceable outside Europe, and are enforceable even in Europe only in those states that have incorporated the Convention into their own legal systems. The very expression '*European* Convention on *Human* Rights' is an oxymoron.

To sum up so far: there are *in fact* no rights or freedoms that are universal across all cultures. The UDHR purports to create them, with corresponding duties on governments even of non-signatory states, but these are in reality no more than aspirations stated as facts. The very concept of universal rights was described by the utilitarian philosopher Jeremy Bentham as 'nonsense on stilts.' Islam also seeks to realise universal moral absolutes.

2.1.2 'Human' rights are unenforceable

There is a further problem with the UDHR. If we tell people that they are entitled to what, in reality, they cannot have, what has been achieved? Article 23 states: 'Everyone has the right to work.' Article 25 states:

> Everyone has the right to a standard of living adequate for the health and well-being of himself and of his family, including food, clothing, housing and medical care and

necessary social services, and the right to security in the event of unemployment, sickness, disability, widowhood, old age or other lack of livelihood in circumstances beyond his control.

But if I proclaim these entitlements in, say, a Somali refugee camp, what response could I expect?

Not only are such rights unenforceable in states that have not created them by legislation, they are also unenforceable against the weight of informal public opinion. As we saw in chapter 1, Mill regarded such social pressure as more of a threat to freedom even than officious legislation. In mid-nineteenth century, middle-class London, that was doubtless truer than it is today, but it is still a very powerful force. Imagine trying to enforce a woman's equal right to employment in a traditional patriarchy. Or instance what happened when federal legislation outlawed Jim Crow racial segregation in the southern United States in the 1960s: segregation was maintained in schools in some Southern states in defiance of the law. Federal troops had to be sent in to enforce it, escorting black children through white mobs into 'white' schools, leading to violent clashes. Even legislated rights may be ignored if sufficiently unpopular. In France, legislation forbidding smoking in public places was widely ignored for years. (Rigorous new measures are now proposed, extending to 'neutral packaging' from 2016; these are opposed by some on the political right.) But perhaps the most deadly informal pressures today are those directed through the social networking websites. Rights are unenforceable against anonymous 'trolls', and against assailants in other jurisdictions.

The concept of rights is essentially a juridical one, so rights that are unenforceable are meaningless. Arguably, to tell people that they have rights they cannot enforce is cruel.

2.1.3 'Human' rights cause tensions in international relations

Further, we may note that the construction of universal absolutes, whether rights, freedom, *sharia* or any other, creates problems for international relations and foreign policy. We have seen that, by asserting that the citizens of non-signatory countries have rights, the UDHR purports to impose corresponding duties on the governments of such countries to recognise and protect those rights. But what gives the signatory states of the UDHR the right to purport to create rights and duties in non-signatory states? Why should non-signatory governments accept such alien duties? The governments of non-signatory states may reasonably fear that their citizens are being stirred up to revolt to claim their alleged rights, and that fear may lead non-democratic governments to crack down ever more fiercely on any signs of independent thinking or demand for rights. Tiananmen Square still focuses this issue.

This perception was confirmed at the 25th Session of the United Nations Human Rights Committee at Geneva in March 2014, when the Russian Foreign Ministry issued this statement:

> Western delegations continue their attempts to use the Human Rights Committee in their unilateral interests in order to exert pressure on some dissenting states with the help of hypocritical accusations of human rights' violations. Such approaches undermined the credibility of the Council and did not contribute to real improvement of the human rights situation at the local level.

Despite this, the Russian Foreign Ministry notes, during the last session, that the Council managed to reach joint decisions on many important issues of promoting and protecting

human rights: 'The Russian delegation has actively partici-
pated in the search for mutually acceptable solutions, pur-
sued a balanced and constructive line aimed at de-
politicization of the human rights sphere and strengthening
the Council's capacity of promoting equitable and mutually
respectful co-operation.' This gives a balanced picture: the
ideal of human rights has indeed gained some recognition in
spite of the perception of it as hypocritical cover for Western
agendas, even if that recognition is the tribute paid by vice to
virtue (a proverbial description of hypocrisy).

Paradoxically, to purport to impose duties on non-signatory states is to deny their right to self-determination. The
UDHR can seem, from the point of view of such states, to be
a 'Declaration of No-Rights'. Similarly, why should non-Isla-
mic states accept *sharia*?

The same applies if freedom is constructed as a universal
absolute. If a country committed to freedom as a universal
norm sees people in a foreign dictatorship denied their
freedom, it sees those people as robbed of what was rightfully theirs. If the people rise to claim their freedom, can it
maintain that all men are born free and also stand by and
watch the freedom movement being crushed? On the other
hand, has it the right to intervene in the internal conflicts of a
sovereign state? Since the state is free as well as its people,
would it even be consistent with the notion of freedom to do
so? The USA in particular has put itself in this quandary by its
statement that freedom is an universal right: had the framers
of the Declaration of Independence confined themselves to
the freedom of *their own* citizens, the USA would not be in
this bind. A nation that really believes in a universal right to
life and liberty will rely primarily on the power of example,
and then on diplomacy, trade, and sporting and cultural
exchanges to introduce its beliefs and practices to the citizens of other states.

In effect, constructing norms as universal absolutes is a

28

recipe for international conflict. Any state can give specific freedoms and rights to some or all of its own citizens. No state or group of states can do these things for *other* sovereign states. Insofar as the UDHR purports to do this, it could perhaps even be seen as illegal under international law.

To state the paradox in another way, all such constructs appear as universal absolutes within the culture that holds them. But to others looking on from other cultures, they appear as relative.

We have seen that there are three objections to the very concept of human, or universal, rights: they do not exist; they are unenforceable and therefore meaningless; and they create international tensions because they do not allow for cultural diversity. Ideally, all references to 'human rights' by organisations, whether international, such as the United Nations Human Rights Committee, statutory, such as the UK Equality and Human Rights Commission, or voluntary, such as Liberty, should be changed to 'citizen rights'. By defining themselves in terms of reality, rather than of aspiration stated as fact, they would gain both focus and credibility. Similarly, the UDHR should be reframed to express the commitment of signatory states to recognising and strengthening the rights of *their own* citizens, and to making them enforceable through their national legal systems, including independent judicatures. States could legislate minimum rights for aliens, whether within the jurisdiction or not. This would prevent another Guantanamo Bay.

In our quest for a definition of a free country, then, it is not open to us to distinguish freedom from rights on the basis that rights are culturally relative and freedom is a universal absolute. Both are in fact culturally relative.

2.2 What is the relationship between freedom and rights in general?

In seeking to define what constitutes a free country, we need to distinguish freedom from rights in general, not just from human rights. To do this, we will enquire more closely into the origins and nature of the concepts of freedom and rights in more recent times, and then into the nature of rights. If you want to skip the history, go straight to Section 2.2.2 to follow the argument.

2.2.1 How did we get here?

Magna Carta (1215) arose out of disputes between the king, the nobles and the Church. It addressed particular abuses, and its scope was national, not universal. It made no grand statements of absolute principle or universal application. It is not even clear whether it applied only to freemen. But it has been regarded over the centuries as asserting the general principle that sovereign power is limited by the liberties of the subject. It sees these liberties as acknowledged by the Crown, not necessarily as inherent in natural law. As well as addressing specific issues, it asserted:

> No Free-man shall be taken, or imprisoned, or dis-possessed, of his free tenement, or liberties, or free customs, or be outlawed, or exiled, or in any way destroyed; nor will we condemn him, nor will we commit him to prison, excepting by the legal judgment of his peers, or by the laws of the land.

What Magna Carta still does for us today is to outline the structure of the social contract between the ruler and the ruled. The ruler undertakes to maintain order, 'The King's Peace', to protect the citizen's freedom to go about his lawful business without hindrance and without being put in fear. We shall see in chapter 5 that that is the essential function of government in a free country. The seeds of this view can be detected in Anglo-Saxon culture before the Norman Conquest, but for our purposes Magna Carta is where it begins. So although we have to read Magna Carta in its historical context, it has been used to shape the social contract in a way essential to any society that would call itself free.

Over the eight centuries that have passed since then, there have been many struggles to keep governments to that role; they continue today and they always will, but Magna Carta's basic structure of the social contract remains. Sir Edward Coke (d. 1634) risked his post as Chief Justice, and perhaps his head, by declaring that even the king was subject to the law: 'Magna Charta is such a fellow, that he will have no sovereign', he wrote, declaring too that even Acts of Parliament would be void if in violation of 'common right and reason'. Coke would approve of my proposal in chapter 16. 'There [in Magna Carta], clearly recognisable, was the rule of law in embryo' said the late Lord Bingham, one of the most respected Law Lords of recent times.* This means that no one, not even rulers or government, is above the law. Only when that is true in fact can the law protect the citizen from all abuse; only then can citizens be truly free.

(The Declaration of Rights of 1689 was in effect the closure of the Civil War. It was primarily an invitation to William and Mary jointly to assume the throne and establish a Protestant succession. It was essentially a division of power between Crown and Parliament, which is why Thomas Paine, in *The Rights of Man*, called it not a Bill of Rights but 'a bill of wrongs, and of insult'.)

It was the English philosopher John Locke in the seventeenth century who expanded the principle that civil society

---

* Bingham, T., *The Rule of Law*, Penguin, 2010.

exists for the protection of the freedom of the individual to imply that all are born free and equal. (The idea of equality Locke took from Richard Hooker, an Elizabethan bishop and one of the finest minds of the English Reformation.) Locke's view of freedom as the 'natural' condition of man led to the need for permanent institutions to ensure that the state did indeed protect it. Thomas Paine, in *The Rights of Man* (1791 & 1792), was the first in modern times to formulate this line of thinking in terms of rights. As noted, he was influential in the process that led up to the drafting of the American Declaration of Independence and the Constitution. After a preamble enumerating grievances against the British Crown, the Declaration begins with the sublime statement at the head of this chapter. This represents a clear articulation of Hooker's, Locke's and Paine's views, and of the ancient concept of natural law.

The American Declaration strongly influenced the French Revolution. American ideas and ideals were taken to France by Paine, and by French officers and soldiers who had been in America to help in the fight against the common enemy, the British. They were captivated by the vision of freedom for all, from any tyranny, guaranteed in a written constitution. The Declaration of the Rights of Man and of Citizens adopted by the French National Assembly after the revolution is clearly based on the American Declaration of Independence, showing Paine's influence. Its first article begins:

1   Men are born, and always continue, free, and equal in respect of their rights.

The Revolution made it clear that power is never voluntarily surrendered, so revolution was the only way to secure freedom and rights for all equally. The vision was caught throughout Europe, and the nineteenth century saw a series of revolutions culminating in the Russian uprising of 1917.

The UK had in effect had its revolution in the Civil War in the seventeenth century, destroying the divine right of kings, securing parliamentary power, government by consent and 'no taxation without representation'.

If a distinction between freedom and rights is beginning to emerge, it is that, whereas rights and freedoms are granted and can be withdrawn by governments, freedom is – or is not – *acknowledged* by governments (often compelled) as the natural condition of all their citizens, which they must always protect. Whereas rights and freedoms are each defined and negotiated or granted separately, one by one, freedom, in the sense in which we are using it here, is acknowledged as the indivisible, basic and inalienable condition of all citizens. Therefore all the state's institutions and laws exist to protect and enlarge that freedom.

2.2.2 Freedom or rights: which should be the basis of the social contract?

Now let us look a little more closely at the concept of rights in general, especially when they form the basis of the social contract. The essential feature of a right is that it is always a right *against* someone. A right creates an equal and opposite duty in someone else. We can see the defining ingredient of rights as a claim or entitlement. This is not true of freedom. Freedom is about *my* actions (or inactions); rights require *other people's* actions (or inactions). Rights may create duties in anyone, particularly anyone with power, such as employers and landlords, but in the context of 'human' rights, they are thought of principally as creating duties, or responsibilities, in government, national and local.

In a country whose social contract and polity are based on a notion of citizens as entitled, as of right, to a range of benefits to be provided by the state, the citizen is relieved of ultimate responsibility for providing for his own needs and for those of his dependants. That responsibility rests ultimately on the government, which is then responsible not only for the safety but also for the welfare of the citizen. The state *must* then fix the level of benefits and other matters, and so dictate the terms of the citizen's life, including his rights, his standard of living and the degree of privacy he may enjoy, in a way no freedom-loving government would countenance. So, counterintuitively but logically, a rights-based polity leads eventually to dependent citizens and a paternal, centralised, all-powerful state. A polity based on the freedom of the individual citizen has the opposite effect: responsibility and power remain with the citizen. Not only are rights and freedom different things; when they form the basis of a country's polity or social contract, they lead to opposite results.

A further risk in a polity based on rights and general dependence on the state is the atrophy of people's initiative, the most vital resource of any economy. If people are entitled to state provision and security from the cradle to the grave, is there a risk of enfeebling their natural self-reliance and enterprise? Entitlement creates dependence. Adam Smith observed: 'Nothing tends so much to corrupt and enervate and debase the mind as dependency, and none gives such noble and generous notions of probity as freedom and independency' (Lectures on Jurisprudence, 28/3/1763, OUP).

A certain degree of social security is indeed essential to any society that would call itself civilised, but is it possible to be too secure? If an employee, for example a clerk in an office of local or national government, has in effect a job for life, may that not in time engender a sloppy incompetence, and a complacent contempt for the very people the office exists to serve? The possibility of losing employment concentrates the mind. The 'right' to security of employment is not absolute but relative; it has to be balanced, like all other rights, against the needs and rights of others, and is therefore a matter of degree. How much security is too much? It is too much when it diminishes the rights of others.

As we shall see in chapter 6, a main function of the state is to protect and enlarge the freedom of the individual citizen. The freedom perspective defines the size and role of the state. In a free country, this is limited to providing (or ensuring the provision of) anything that will protect or enlarge the citizen's freedom, and will therefore reduce dependence, such as education and health provision.

If what we may call an 'entitlement culture' leads to dependence and to a powerful and paternal state, in what ways is a free country different? Do the citizens of a free country not have entitlements? They do, and more. Where freedom is stated in a constitution to be the default condition of every citizen, as in the USA, that necessarily contains within it the idea of entitlement. In a genuinely free country, the individual is guaranteed her rights in a legally enforceable form as a part of that freedom. Freedom is large: it *contains* rights, entitlements and discrete freedoms in a form that does not deprive or relieve the citizen of responsibility, but rather enhances it; a form which minimises dependency. The only *intrinsic* claim a citizen has on the government of a free country is that given by Magna Carta, the right to freedom protected and enlarged by the state under the rule of law. All other claims on government are, in a free country, matters of variable political contract, not of constitution.

We have seen that, when considered as the basis of a constitution or of the social contract, freedom and rights lead to opposite results. There are other differences. For example, in a free country, the assumption is that the citizen is free to do anything that is not specifically forbidden by law, so in a criminal trial the accused is assumed innocent unless proved guilty of a specified offence beyond a reasonable doubt, to the satisfaction of a jury: the burden of proof is on the prosecution. In a system based on legislated rights, the implied assumption is reversed. The citizen is permitted only the listed activities, and there can then be a tendency to transfer the burden of proof on to the defendant to prove that his action falls within the listed rights.

For all the reasons advanced in this chapter, a declaration of freedom is preferable to a declaration of rights as the basis of a country's polity.

There is a political risk here. A polity based on universal entitlements appeals to those who wish to stand up for the poor, the oppressed and the marginalised, to those whose primary value is social justice, to left-leaning people. A polity based on freedom will appeal to those who are interested in living their own life, building a business or making a fortune. The political right is very discontented with talk of rights, whether 'human' or European, but it seems to have forgotten that freedom is the alternative to rights, and that freedom has always been central to its own best traditions. The freedom issue shows whether any political party is dominated by its libertarian or its authoritarian wing.

Theoretically, one merit of the republican view of freedom, noted in chapter 1, is that it makes freedom an acceptable and attractive concept to the left even more than to the right, and at least shows that the right has no monopoly of the value of freedom. Historically, British people across all parties have been ready to defend their freedom against all threats, domestic or foreign, but there is a risk that the issue could become politicised along party lines, the left insisting on rights and entitlements as the basic relationship between citizens and the state, and the right defending freedom as the basis of that relationship. Freedom is a constitutional issue, even a human one, and it is in the interests of all parties to ensure that it is always a cross-party, free-vote issue. This is especially important at times when freedom is under threat, as it is now. Thus it is encouraging that there is a cross-party Parliamentary Joint Committee on Human Rights which scrutinises prospective bills for compatibility with human rights legislation. How much influence it has is unclear. It would be better if the focus was freedom, but it does focus the issue in a cross-party context.

Campaigning organisations such as Liberty need to be very careful not to appear to be infiltrated or captured by any one political party or tendency. Shami Chakrabarti, the Director of Liberty, made this point in an interview with *The Sunday Times* on 8 June 2014: she finds libertarians and authoritarians in all parties. It would be tragic if Liberty could even be suspected of partisanship.

These two mindsets seem to occur in all cultures, polarising in times of crisis. Among the Chinese about 2,500 years ago, in a time of violent social chaos, it was Confucius for authority and the Tao, in effect, for freedom. Among the Greeks, it was the Apollonians and the Dionysiacs. There will always be both: we have to abstract the best from each. The traditional way of doing this in the UK is the adversarial system, as in elections, courts of law and in the very furnishing of the Houses of Parliament: not circular, as at the United Nations, but two sides facing each other.

An example of the authoritarian mindset at its most arrogant was given by Liam Fox, a former Conservative defence secretary, in an interview reported in the *Guardian* of 22 June 2014. In the context of radicalised Muslims returning to this country from the Syrian conflict, he said: '... it is a genuine debate in a democracy, between the libertarians who say the state must not get too powerful and pretty much the rest of us who say the state must protect itself'. Dr Fox wishes us to see libertarians as a deviant minority undermining defence. That is a gross and dishonest caricature unworthy of a politician.

It is therefore vital at times like the present that organisations such as Liberty, Big Brother Watch, Human Rights Watch and Privacy International should be seen to have very widespread support, even if their focus is rights rather than freedom, so that they cannot be depicted as minority, fringe, subversive, disloyal or cranky elements, and so that their activities are well understood and valued. MPs should be constantly deluged with mail and emails that make it clear to them that their future parliamentary career could depend on their vigilance for our freedom.

While libertarians make common cause across party boundaries, other distinctions can become blurred. We have seen that constitutions (written or unwritten) based on rights and those based on freedom are very different things, leading to very different outcomes. Yet even leading figures in campaigning organisations, among others, often use the terms *freedom* and *rights* as if they were the same thing. Campaigning organisations necessarily watch the detail of legislation for threats to freedom. This is invaluable and essential. But they can then risk missing the big picture, losing the vision of overall freedom, of a free country. Such campaigning organisations do essential and courageous work. National organisations such as Liberty and Big Brother Watch, and internationally Amnesty and Human Rights Watch in particular, do need and deserve widespread support, not just financially but also by people joining the organisation, supporting campaigns and frequently emailing and visiting MPs; '38 Degrees' is a useful and effective campaigning online presence that can quickly raise large petitions relating to freedom, among other causes. These organisations, with the media, are the most effective proactive agents in the field at present. They are 'the good guys' in the constant fight against the abuse of power. The ECHR necessarily focuses the issue in the field of rights; yet it is important to dictate the terms of the issue, not to allow others to do so. Confusing freedom, freedoms and rights, and human rights in particular, does nothing to validate campaigns. An organisation that calls itself Liberty but campaigns mostly for human rights is in danger of confusing its supporters and, while achieving much, still achieving less than it might if it campaigned primarily for a free country.

Perhaps such organisations could devise a strategy to reframe the debate in terms of a constitutional basis of guaranteed individual freedom as a foundation on which to construct citizen rights and freedoms. The 800th anniversary of Magna Carta in 2015 would seem an ideal opportunity to start that process.

However, in contexts other than the social contract, freedom and rights are not mutually exclusive. Once freedom is established as the very basis and purpose of the constitution (accepted as convention if unwritten), there will be a need to specify, define and limit some citizen rights and freedoms. The American Constitution provides us with a useful precedent and model. The basic affirmation of freedom has been supplemented with later amendments, such as the Fourth Amendment specifying a right to privacy. In the UK and the USA there are Freedom of Information Acts to specify the extent and limitations of that freedom.

2.2.3 So what about the Human Rights Act?

In the UK, we are currently governed by the ECHR, which was incorporated into English law by the Human Rights Act 1998 (HRA), and so by the European Court of Human Rights. The court has assumed a legislative power far beyond the judicial function defined in its founding documents, in that it now invents new rights which are then binding on member states and their courts. Many of the judgements of the Court are widely seen in the UK as overly transgressive of national sovereignty, and tend to bring the whole concept of human rights into disrepute. Many, particularly on the political right, wish to repeal the Act and withdraw from the ECHR altogether. The Conservative Party committed itself to doing so if elected, and brought forward proposals for a new Act at its party conference on 3rd October 2014. The proposals repatriate some sovereignty, but vaguely exclude rights from 'trivial' matters, leaving open the question of who defines 'trivial'. There are also problems relating to devolved authorities. Citizen rights are important so long as they are based in freedom as the default condition of citizens. Such an Act would not make a modern Magna Carta redundant. Rather, the two should be related.

Legal advice from within the Ministry of Justice has stated that it is not legally possible to withdraw from the ECHR without withdrawing from the EU altogether.

On the other side are many who see the Act as their only or main protection against the abuse of power. At times like the present, this is hardly surprising. Such people point to a number of judgements of the European Court of Human Rights that preserved a British citizen's rights or freedoms when the UK courts failed to do so, and to the erosion of constitutional safeguards, as we shall see in chapter 5. Such people will fight to keep the Act, rightly and understandably, although a modern Magna Carta with specified citizen rights on a basis of individual freedom would be a better outcome.

The widespread resentment of the ECHR is dangerous if it gives those who want a strong (even if 'minimal') state an excuse to limit or attenuate human rights and therefore freedom also. Those who will campaign to keep the Act may reasonably fear that repeal might trigger an authoritarian backlash that would damage not only rights, but freedom itself. An example of such a backlash was a proposed new school curriculum which would exclude any mention of human rights. Liberty submitted reasons for reversing that, and was successful. It would be even better if *freedom* was fully developed as a major theme in our history syllabus and national identity. That would be British at its best, and lay essential foundations for freedom in the next generation.

Whether the HRA remains or is repealed or replaced, a

foundation of freedom is needed: a need precisely matched by a modern Magna Carta.

2.3 Summary

To sum up the main points of this chapter so far:

- there are no 'human', or universal, rights, only citizen rights;
- nor are all people born free;
- rights that are not enforceable are meaningless;
- some states and groups of states construct rights, freedom or submission to god as universal norms;
- constructing universal norms creates problems for international relations;
- freedom and rights when seen as universal values only make sense in the state that holds them, but look culturally relative to other states and cultures;
- rights and freedoms are granted by governments and can be abridged or withdrawn by them;
- freedom as the basic condition of its citizens is acknowledged, not granted, by governments;
- a social contract based on rights leads to dependency and an all-powerful state, one based on the freedom of the citizen to the opposite;
- a constitutional guarantee of freedom automatically includes rights;
- such a guarantee is preferable to a list of rights as a basis for a constitution;
- on a basis of freedom, specific freedoms and rights will be enacted;
- freedom underpins the presumption of innocence;
- the curricula of schools in a free country will emphasise freedom, especially in the history syllabus.

2.4 A modern Magna Carta?

In the UK, whether or not we opt out of the ECHR and the European Court of Human Rights (and the EU), we urgently need a rigorous modern version of Magna Carta, guaranteeing the freedom of every citizen. It would be a wonderful way to celebrate its 800th anniversary in 2015, and a way to repatriate some sovereignty. Surely any freedom-loving party or government would want at the very least to take advice publicly on the legal implications of such a step, to consult widely and to act unless there was some insuperable obstacle? The work of the Joint Parliamentary Committee on Constitutional Reform makes a good starting point. A tentative list of possible contents of a modern Magna Carta is offered for thought and discussion at the end of this work, in chapter 16.

There are distractions. The fall-out from the Scottish referendum focuses constitutional attention on devolution to both Scotland and other regions in the UK, and marginal parliamentary reform. It is unfortunate that 2015 is also the year of a general election that absorbs the attention of the media for some months. Yet the issues discussed here are fundamental, and likely to be far-reaching. The ideal would be the initiation of a process, such as a Royal Commission, to create momentum and increase the likelihood of the new government giving the issue the priority it deserves.

Whether this country would also want to withdraw from the UDHR is another matter. Though consistency might suggest it, and however meaningless the 'rights' stated, withdrawal might send a very different message about this country from the message that would be sent by withdrawing from the ECHR and enacting a modern Magna Carta.

Meanwhile, we are likely to be embroiled in the human rights debate for some time to come. One useful discipline might be never to utter or accept a statement of rights unless accompanied by a corresponding statement of duties or (more fashionably) responsibilities: those owed both to and by the holder of the rights.

But a polity, a social contract, based on freedom should be our primary and constant aim.

In our quest for a definition of a free country, we have distinguished freedom from anarchy, from freedom*s*, from independence, from human rights and from rights in general. To make it useful in the twenty-first century, we now explore the wholly new freedom-related issues raised by the technologies of surveillance and information storage and manipulation. Only then will we be in a position to suggest a definition for our own times.

3

Freedom and Privacy: The Media and the Internet

Privacy is an outdated and unneeded concept.
Mark Zuckerberg

Zuckerberg seems to think that privacy is only for billionaires and founders of social networks.
Breda O'Brien, *The Irish Times*

The technology that has liberated us in so many ways is also capable of suffocating that inviolable personal space that once had another name. That name was freedom.
Andrew Sullivan, *The Sunday Times*, 6/3/05

It is our personal privacy that makes each individual unique. Our innermost thoughts, our secrets, our fears and dreams, our values, our distinctive view of the world, are the only things that make us different from everyone else. The more that area is eroded and diminished, the fewer unique features remain to each individual, the more we become mere cells in the general amorphous mass, or numbers on a list. Diversity dies, and, in the logical extreme, we become indistinguishable from a colony of ants or bees, except that we would be less cohesive and purposeful. Brave New World beckons.

44

What are the current threats to our privacy? And do they affect our freedom? We look first at the threats.

3.1 Threats to privacy

3.1.1 Online surveillance

Edward Snowdon's disclosures of the Prism, Tempora and the American National Security Agency (NSA) XKeyscore programmes, used by the governments of the USA and the UK to harvest secretly *all* internet traffic, did not even come as a surprise. If we are no longer surprised when we learn that we are being spied upon, our lack of surprise and reaction shows how institutionalised we have already become: we want to feel comfortable and safe, never mind about privacy. But the revelations are still shocking.

The collaboration between the NSA and the British equivalent (GCHQ) is useful to both. The NSA cannot – in theory – intercept internal communications (those both originating and delivered in the USA) because of the Fourth Amendment to the Constitution, which guarantees privacy. The British agency, which according to one of its own emails has a lighter regime, might also wish to avoid a possible political backlash from any revelation of internal surveillance. But both are empowered to intercept *external* communications - that is, any originating or delivered abroad. So each can intercept the other's internal communications and then trade the results. We shall look further at this in chapter 6 on freedom and security.

So it goes much wider than the USA and the UK. Snowden revealed that the NSA does not only secretly collect the communications of its own people, but that it invades the sovereignty and privacy of other nations by collecting their communications also: that is, communications both originated *and* delivered abroad, not only of companies and individuals but also governments. The president of Germany, Herr Joachim Gauck, has commented: 'The fear that our telephone calls and mails are being collated and saved by foreign intelligence services narrows the feeling of freedom and with that in turn comes the danger that freedom itself is impaired.' Poignantly, he added: 'I never would have thought that the fear could arise again in Germany, that private communication is no longer possible' (source: *The Irish Times Weekend*, 27–28/7/13).

As more of the Snowden files are released, the picture gets even worse. *The Guardian* newspaper reported on 27 February 2014:

> GCHQ files dating between 2008 and 2010 explicitly state that a surveillance programme codenamed Optic Nerve collected still images of Yahoo webcam chats in bulk and saved them to agency databases, regardless of whether individual users were an intelligence target or not. In one six-month period in 2008 alone, the agency collected webcam imagery – including substantial quantities of sexually explicit communications – from more than 1.8 million Yahoo user accounts globally.

Indeed, Vodafone, in its Law Enforcement Disclosure Report of June 2014, revealed that government agencies in at least 29 countries have direct access to its traffic through secret wires which can be used without a warrant. Stephen Deadman, Vodafone's group privacy officer, has commented: 'These pipes exist, the direct access model exists ... Without an official warrant, there is no external visibility' – which is just what government agencies want. 'The fact that a government has to issue a piece of paper is an important constraint on how powers are used'. (Source: *The Irish Times*, 7/6/14).

This confirms that security agencies not only intercept communications. They can and do penetrate computers protected by passwords and collect any information stored there, including passwords and bank account details. No privacy at all is respected, even that of communication between solicitor and client. Knowledge of that gives a prosecution a large and unfair advantage, derailing justice.

It is not just the American and British security agencies that have developed the habit of universal surveillance. The European Commission has plans to mandate the installation in all new cars of event data recorders (EDRs). These continually record the location of the car with other information. This would help police to track suspect vehicles, and insurance companies to adapt premiums according to the driving habits of customers. But it could also help criminal hackers to gain access to the information and use it to track victims – for robbery, for example. The principle is the same: the movements of the citizen are monitored.

We shall see in chapter 6 that, under some circumstances, such comprehensive surveillance might be justified by security needs. But even if it is, that does not mean that the Fourth Amendment, and rights to privacy in other countries, are abolished. The issue of the relationship between privacy and security will be considered in chapter 6; the constitutional implications in chapter 5. Here, we remain focused on the relationship between privacy and freedom, or the status of privacy in a free country, with a view to refining a definition of a free country for the digital age in chapter 4. We shall see how and why a loss of privacy is also a loss of freedom.

Further, when we know we are being watched, even the most innocent – perhaps especially they – are careful to avoid choices that might be misinterpreted or give rise to suspicion. Thus the knowledge of being surveyed reduces the choices available to us.

But many people are unaware of the extent of surveillance and of the information held on them. If we are unaware of it, does it matter? If we can go on doing what we want to do happily unaware of being watched and recorded, are we not still free? No. The reverse is true. If we know we are being watched, we can choose to react in some way, such as avoidance. If we are not aware of being watched, we are deprived of that choice and are therefore less free.

And when we discover that our supposedly private communications have been taken – in effect, stolen – by others, the impact of this violation can be very damaging.

However, surveillance is not the only possible mode of online relationship between government and people. On 3 July 2014, the news page of India.com reported that the Indian Prime Minister Narendra Modi, who describes himself as 'an avid user' of online social networks, had had talks with Sheryl Sandberg, the chief operating officer of Facebook, with a view to using Facebook as an instrument of government. On his page, he wrote: 'A platform such as Facebook can be used for governance and better interaction between the people and governments.' This seems a very enlightened and positive approach. However, because of the power imbalance, it is important to think through some of the implications. If government uses Facebook to disseminate official information, that would disenfranchise those who choose not to use Facebook, so would it become compulsory to have a profile on Facebook? Then everybody's communications and details would become available to government. In India, it would be necessary to accelerate programmes to bring millions online, an immense project with which Facebook is eager to help. As always, the possibilities for both good and ill seem limitless, the ramifications complex and the consequences largely unpredictable. Governments will experiment, and democrats and libertarians will remain vigilant, especially for the rule of law.

3.1.2 Police surveillance

One of the shocking aspects of Prism, Tempora and XKey-score is their universality. Everyone is watched. A more local example of total, or totalitarian, surveillance occurred in the UK. The small market town of Royston in Hertfordshire was surrounded in 2011 by cameras covering every road in and out of the town. These cameras read the registration number of every vehicle entering or leaving the town, which was then stored for at least two years. It was impossible to enter or leave the town in a vehicle without being recorded. The Information Commissioner's Office (ICO) ruled this unlawful on the ground that the measures taken must be proportionate to the problem addressed, and that the constabulary had carried out no adequate impact assessment before introducing the cameras. It was difficult to see how a small market town needed such measures. The ICO only carried out the review because of the initiative of organisations vigilant for freedom and privacy: (No CCTV, Big Brother Watch and Privacy International), which shows the necessity and value of such organisations.

The police, on the other hand, sought to justify their practice on the grounds that it made Royston the safest town in the country because it deterred criminals from entering it. No statistics or other evidence were offered to support this assertion. The statistics showed no significant change in crime levels when the cameras were installed. They have since been switched off, and no significant change occurred then either.

Nor does the police response address the issue in a balanced way. The police actually boasted of a 'Ring of Steel', which sounds like a prison. How did the residents of Royston regard it? Were they consulted? Such policies and attitudes make it increasingly difficult to see the police as protectors of the citizen's freedom, and tend to legitimate the views of those who see the police as an enemy. If that polarisation, already familiar in parts of our inner cities, becomes more widespread, it is fatal to freedom. It heralds a police state. (Source: *Cambridge News*, 25/07/13.)

3.1.3 Press, commercial and other surveillance

The state is not the only threat to freedom and privacy. The media have an equivocal role in the freedom debate. On one hand, the technology is available to reporters to violate the privacy of individuals for commercial purposes: the Milly Dowler case will always be remembered as a gross example, but it is by no means unique. On the other hand, free media are an essential bulwark of freedom. Many an abuse of power has been exposed in this way.

The Leveson Inquiry represented an attempt to have the best of both worlds: control of abuse with freedom of speech. But the resulting debate shows yet again that there are limits to what governments can do. The only way to have both freedom of speech and freedom from abuse (by both politicians and journalists) is to create a truly free country, where a passion for freedom and respect is widespread across society. The ballot box and market forces respectively will then ensure the balance that is consistent with freedom

On the credit side, a vigorous, investigative press is essential to freedom. But such newspapers are under threat from online news sources. Newspapers are experiencing diminishing circulation and advertising revenue, and investigative journalism is expensive. If newspapers reach the point where they can no longer afford investigative reporting, abuses of power, and therefore the attenuation of freedom, will expand, checked only by the judiciary, whose role is reactive, not proactive like that of the media.

State agencies and media investigators are not the only agents to penetrate our privacy. In London, in the summer of

2013, it was found that rubbish bins standing by streets had been fitted with hidden apparatus that could pull information out of the smartphones of passers-by without their knowledge. So far as I know, it has not been revealed who installed that apparatus, or how they intended to use the information. Similarly, Facebook can have access to connected phones, even using their cameras without the owner's knowledge.

Criminals can steal our identities, our bank and credit card details and other information. Private individuals also can use smartphones to identify and locate people covertly. It is easy to buy covert surveillance equipment; it is possible to take control of someone's computer including any webcam, and then post intimate photographs or sound files on the web. These abuses are possible because of the anonymity of the web. It is easy to hide behind a false email address and profile on networking sites. This allows horrific attacks by internet trolls on entirely innocent people. School-age bullying online can drive young people to suicide. 'Revenge pornography', when people post online compromising explicit pictures of former lovers, has become so common that the government considered legislation to address just that evil, even though adequate legislation already exists.

According to a report by Murad Ahmed in *The Times* of 19 May 2014, encryption to hide identity is fast increasing across the world as a reaction to revelations of surveillance. In Europe, it quadrupled in a year to 6.1 per cent of all traffic; in North America it increased from 2.3 to 3.8 per cent and in Latin America from 1.8 to 10.4 per cent.

Does the anonymity give freedom? Not in such cases, because it enables behaviour without responsibility, and we have seen that that is not freedom but anarchy. This confirms that our definition of a free country must include individual responsibility as an integral component.

(It is possible that anonymity will soon become impossible. Providers are experimenting with biometric recognition, such as fingerprints, not to make anonymity impossible but as a form of security thought to be better than that provided by passwords. Individual users would then become identifiable. Alongside the good effects, there might be adverse ones. Such a system would be ideal for dictators wishing to identify dissidents. For a fuller discussion of the issues and studies of anonymity on the web, see the journal *New Scientist*, 26/10/13, pp. 34ff.)

3.1.4 Stored information

Online and other surveillance is one way our personal information can be harvested. A further issue is the use and abuse of information once stored, however it was acquired. Government agencies, social networks and other commercial companies hold huge amounts of our information, much of it gained legally or with our (more or less informed) consent.

We noted in chapter 1 that Google's mission to make all information available to all people appeared to ignore legitimate needs for secrecy, privacy and confidentiality. So simplistic and unrealistic was it that it invites speculation on other possible agendas. Since it involved Google processing the information, it could, for example, be read as a bid to control all information. As we shall see, information is power. This was graphically demonstrated by Facebook in 2012. It filtered the news feeds of 689,003 users, some for positive matter and some for negative, and then monitored the posts of those users to see whether the tone of the news feeds influenced their mood. Facebook's conclusion: 'Emotions expressed by friends, via online social networks, influence our own moods ... evidence for massive-scale emotional contagion via social networks.'

This raises several issues. First, the users were unaware that their news feeds were being manipulated. They gave no consent, even by signing the small-print terms and conditions of service: research was not written into those until four months later. Such contempt for ethical issues indicates the arrogance of excessive power: perhaps Mark Zuckerberg considers ethics an 'outdated and unneeded concept' – like privacy.

More significant still, consider how such power could be used to manipulate the perceptions and the passions of millions of people. 'Emotional contagion' indeed. Who controls the world's information controls the world. (Sources: Proceedings of the National Academy of Sciences (American), issue of March 2014; Davin O'Dwyer in *The Irish Times*, 5/7/14).

Even if we have no internet connection, our information is stored, perhaps without our knowledge, on hard drives in computers that are connected to the internet. That means everyone who has ever used health services, everyone with a bank account, everyone who pays taxes and everyone who has a passport or a driving licence has personal information stored in computers that are accessible not only to large numbers of unknown but authorised people, but also to unauthorised people, to surveillance by government agencies (which may share information), and to hackers and criminals.

The UK National Health Service (NHS) holds much personal information on millions of people. On the one hand, the NHS is desperate for funds; on the other hand, it is in possession of this mass of information which could be sold for enough to ease its financial problems. Under these circumstances, managers under pressure will inevitably seek ways to monetise at least some of that information. The result was the CARE.data initiative, under which some patient information was to be sold to insurance actuaries. The information was said to be completely anonymous, but on examination it appeared that it might be traceable to identifiable patients in some cases. The presentation of the scheme for consultation appeared to lack honesty.

Similarly, the UK tax authority (HMRC) has a mass of very saleable information. It has drawn up plans that would allow the personal financial data of the UK's taxpayers to be released to third parties as with the NHS's CARE.data initiative. The draft legislation would allow information relating to millions of taxpayers to be sold to private companies and public bodies if there is deemed to be a public benefit. HMRC has already launched a pilot programme where it has released information relating to VAT registration to three credit ratings agencies: Equifax, Experian and Dun & Bradstreet. (Source: Wired.co.uk, 19/4/14).

Government is a relative latecomer in waking up to the potential market value of personal information. It is regularly harvested in enormous quantities and sold for profit by big internet companies such as Google and Facebook. Loyalty card schemes yield vast amounts of information about customers' shopping preferences: precisely the kind of information for which advertisers and merchandisers will pay well. It is even said that Tesco's Clubcard scheme holds information of greater value than Facebook's.

Companies selling goods and services have access to our credit records. Insurance companies would like access to our health records. Transport for London records the movements of users of its Oyster card. Credit card companies record the place, date and even the time of all card transactions.

Do we have any control at all over our own information? The debate was focused in May 2014 by the judgement of the European Court of Justice (ECJ) in the case of Mario Costeja Gonzalez. Mr Gonzalez was troubled by Google referencing his name to an old and short report in *La Vanguardia* newspaper in 1998, just 36 words long, which reported his house as being repossessed at that time. Many years later, this was causing him serious difficulties. Google refused to take it down, so he went to court. The Spanish judges asked the ECJ for guidance, and the ECJ ruled that Google was under the same obligations as public authorities and must remove any information that was inadequate, irrelevant or no longer relevant. There is a 'right to be forgotten'.

This judgement is at first sight laudably protective of the individual's right to control his own information, to protect his privacy, against the overwhelming power of Google, which has 93 per cent of the searches carried out in Europe. But it has some paradoxical aspects and results. *La Vanguardia* can still carry the piece in its archive: it is just that Google cannot have access to it. The judgement has no effect outside Europe, so a user using a service provider based in, say, the USA, can still see the piece. Indeed, by using Google. com rather than a national version (such as Google.co.uk), any computer anywhere can gain access, though the legality of this has yet to be tested. Strangest of all, this was not like a case where the information was of a private or personal nature: it was a matter of public record anyway.

Juridically, the judgement raises more basic issues. There is no appeal from the ECJ: it is the final court of appeal, so Google then had to work out some way to implement the judgement. It conferred on Google powers of censorship which it insists it does not want. It is refusing to take down material on public figures because there is a public interest in it. This is based on the Gonzalez judgement, which states that individuals have a fundamental right to privacy that is greater than the need to provide information to the public, but that that right can be breached for specific reasons 'such as the role played by the data subject in public life'. This still leaves Google, and other search engines and ISPs, to decide on individual cases. Some posts have been taken down and then restored. It is not clear where any appeal from such decisions would lie (see *The Sunday Times*, 29/6/14).

Immediately after the judgement was delivered, more than 1,000 people invoked it to require Google to take down embarrassing information. In *The Sunday Times* of 18 May

2014, John Kampfner suggested that this could include a convicted paedophile, a surgeon who has received a critical review, an MP whose expenses claims are under scrutiny and others with something to hide. This is indeed true. As Emma Carr of Big Brother Watch put it, 'the principle that you have a right to be forgotten is a laudable one, but it was never intended to be a way for people to rewrite history'. The Data Retention and Investigation Powers Act 2014 (DRIPA) is a response to this judgement.

Kampfner pays lip service to the right to privacy, and to the need and right of offenders to delete 'spent' convictions in order to rehabilitate, but keeps his emotional firepower for the fight against what he sees as online censorship. 'The internet presaged a brave new world in which citizens could access information at the click of a button, without fear or favour,' he writes.

But the ideal of all information everywhere being available to all people, the original mission of Google, was always fantasy. It ignored obvious needs for personal privacy and for at least some secrecy for those charged with running countries or companies. It also ignored the whole concept of confidentiality, as between doctor and patient, solicitor and client, priest and penitent, journalist and source.

In all offline media, there are legal limitations on the freedom of speech. There are laws against inciting racial hatred, and against blasphemy and obscenity. There are civil remedies for libel and slander. The traditional media are seeking to refine the criterion of public interest to determine the boundary between the rights to privacy and free speech. In theory, personal information can only be used if the public have an interest in knowing it (as distinct from being *interested* in knowing it.) Why is the online world different? Why should the same public interest criterion not apply there? To argue otherwise appears to be arguing not for freedom of speech but for the perpetuation of the internet anarchy we noticed in chapter 1.

The difference is, of course, one of practice, not principle: that there is no one jurisdiction that can establish the rule of law on the whole world-wide web. As we saw in chapter 1, anarchy seems to be set to remain the norm online. The growing use of cyber espionage, both national and commercial, and of cyber warfare, does not bode well.

Apart from the Investigatory Powers Tribunal, our only protection is the Data Protection Act 1998, operated by the Information Commissioner's Office. This gives us the right of access to information held on us. It is important and valuable but it relates to information held on us that we know about. It is impossible to be sure what *other* information is held on us or by whom, whether it is secure or even accurate; much less where it goes and how it is used. We no longer own our personal information.

More fundamentally still, the judgement of the ECJ in the Gonzalez case compels us to enquire into the competence of judges to rule on such technical issues. According to a Reuters report on a case in the USA, 'One US Supreme Court justice referred to Netflix as "Netflick". Another seemed not to know that HBO is a cable channel. A third appeared to think that most software coding could be tossed off in a mere weekend.' We are in a period when the law, and society in general, are struggling to adapt to wholly new issues. 'The jurisprudence established now will have far-reaching implications'. (Source for this paragraph: Davin O'Dwyer's balanced and thoughtful piece in *The Irish Times Weekend*, 17/5/14). The task is daunting: we need judges with technical knowledge – perhaps in the form of assessors sitting with them – to generate confidence.

3.2 Assurances

We are assured that there are sufficient safeguards in place; that the agencies operate within the law; that the volume of online information is so great that it has to be filtered so that only suspect communication is examined; that only metadata are taken (that is, names and dates of correspondents but not the content of emails); that if we are doing nothing wrong, we have nothing to fear.

We would have to be very naive to accept these assurances. The Regulation of Investigatory Powers Act 2000 (RIPA) was an attempt to reassure people that surveillance was subject to the law. Even the use of the Act gives grounds for concern. In 2013, there were no less than 514,608 notices and authorisations under the Act: 88 per cent of these were by police and other law enforcement agencies. (Source: LocalGov.co.uk, 9/4/14). Appeals under the Act go not to an open court of law but to the Investigatory Powers Tribunal, whose members are all judges or senior barristers appointed by the Queen on the advice of persons unspecified, presumably including the prime minister or his appointees – that is, the executive. This appears to be machinery for hearing cases where national security requires secrecy; it is the only place where the citizen can complain about the intelligence services. Its powers are purely investigatory; it appears to have no power to act on its findings or to hold the security services to account. There is no appeal from the IPT, so an unsuccessful complainant may not be told why her complaint was rejected. In chapter 6 on freedom and security, we shall look at the working and the limitations of the RIPA.

Not only does the RIPA allow a lot of surveillance: we cannot trust those who have access to our information. It appears that the police tapped the private communications of the Lawrence family illegally and secretly, in the hope of finding material with which to discredit them, in order to protect officers compromised in their dealings with that shamefully ill-treated family.

Corruption is perceived to be increasing in many sectors of our public life, and there will always be corruptible people among those in possession of 'confidential' information.

In a typically well-informed and lucid piece in *The Sunday Times* of 27 October 2013, Jenni Russell wrote of government surveillance:

> The people who work on the material cannot be trusted to keep to the rules. They are human, which means that some of them will be incompetent, overly curious or venal ... battered women have been tracked down by their partners ... bank employees have illegally accessed others' bank details to use in divorce battles, policemen have tracked and harassed their ex-lovers, health staff have used databases to taunt their rivals ... Two years ago the organisation Big Brother Watch published a report detailing the police's misuse of data. In 2007, 10,904 officers and staff were disciplined and 243 received criminal convictions for accessing or leaking confidential information. In the National Health Service in the three years to 2011 there were at least 800 cases of staff misusing its databases, including two dozen cases where private medical details were posted on social networks

She continues, referring to agents of the state: '... the more information they hold, the more power they have'. The more power *they* have, the less free are *we*.

As if that were not enough, there is also the issue of incompetence. There have been several instances of the private information of millions of people stored unencrypted on discs that have been posted unsecured and lost, left on public transport or found in dustbins.

Even if surveillance did only take metadata, that would still grossly damage many people. Suppose it showed that you had been in touch with a drugs agency, a pregnancy clinic and a debt counselling service. That would be enough to destroy any hopes you might have had of buying life, health or travel insurance or of getting a mortgage or a visa for foreign travel. You might have contacted all those agencies for information for someone else (a daughter?) and have no such concerns for yourself, but the metadata alone would make you unacceptable. You would not even know why you were meeting with refusals or being charged extortionate prices.

If we are doing nothing wrong, we have nothing to fear?

3.3 Privacy and freedom

The assurances we are offered are not only unconvincing: they do not address the basic issue. This is that knowledge is power. When people, organisations or government agencies have knowledge of me – of my communications, my browsing history, my relationships, my activities, my health record, my whereabouts – to that extent they have power over me. Even if that power is never used, or even if it is used benignly, it remains true that the knowledge of my personal life gives power over me to whoever possesses it, as Jenni Russell observed.

The connection between freedom and privacy can be stated thus:

> To the extent that other people have knowledge of me and power over me, to that extent I am less free. Privacy is therefore essential to freedom. A free country will put a high priority on protecting the privacy of the individual citizen.

So how are we to relate freedom of speech as used by the media, and the holding of our information, to the right to privacy? In his piece in *The Sunday Times* mentioned above, John Kampfner constructs the issue as one of balance. He wrote: 'The balance will never be perfect, but I would rather live in a society that veers towards the raucous than the respectful.' That is not the issue: respectfulness is not being advocated, and raucousness is not the problem. Respect for the individual's right to privacy is precisely what is necessary in a free country: it is not the losing side of a balance. Mr Kampfner is a journalist. By constructing the issue as one of balance, and deciding that balance for us, he is able to formulate it in a way that suits his personal and professional interests. That is not to say that his case is without merit, but that it is fatally *un*balanced.

There are other ways to construct the issue that do take better account of both interests. It is grossly simplistic to construct it as a balance between two monolithic blocks, free speech and privacy. The issues are far more nuanced, and each needs to be disaggregated. There are different people and interests involved, and there are different classes of information.

Private individuals living private lives are not in the same position as those who have chosen to live their lives in the public eye, or who actively seek publicity, as the ECJ noted in the Gonzalez case. Similarly, some information is essential to national security or commercial secrecy, other information is trivial gossip. Some is false and damaging, some is true and damaging. Some seems useful but is false, some is useful and true. Not all journalists are interested in these distinctions.

The challenge, therefore, is to devise ways of meeting these needs, not to trade them. The standard developed so far is the public interest test. The right to privacy is the norm, the default presumption. Only that information that people have an interest in knowing can be disclosed. That is not the

61

same thing as being *interested* in knowing. There is some way to go before adequate definitions and methods of enforcement are agreed

The French media until recently unanimously observed a tacit code which respected the privacy of politicians' sexual lives. Indeed French presidents have often been accompanied at public functions and even international occasions by their mistresses. To the foreign eye, it might even seem that the French people would be surprised if a powerful figure did *not* have extra-curricular relationships. Even a public figure was seen as entitled to privacy in his private affairs so long as it did not affect performance in public service.

The Americans showed similar political maturity in 1998, when President Bill Clinton was exposed as having irregular sexual relations with the intern Monica Lewinsky. The puritan tendency joined with opportunistic republicans in an attempt to have Clinton impeached. Eventually, the people decided that Clinton was doing a good job as president, and that this was not affected by his sexual behaviour, however deplorable.

The right to privacy, therefore, is not restricted to private citizens. The ECJ's remark that public figures are less entitled to privacy needs to be developed in a nuanced way. Quite apart from the issue of principle, we are unlikely to attract the most able into government if their lives, and their families' lives, are to be made miserable by constant harassment and intrusion.

What constitutes public interest? And who is to decide? Some cases are clear. If an official in possession of significant information is seduced or blackmailed by an agent of a foreign power, then there is such a public interest. In the 1950s, a junior official in the Admiralty called John Vassall, who was homosexual at a time when such behaviour was still illegal, was trapped by the KGB while on attachment in Moscow, and blackmailed into spying for the Russians. Although junior, both in Moscow and later in London, he was able to supply the Russians with large amounts of crucial technical information which enabled the Soviet navy to modernise. For disclosure to be in the public interest, some such dimension is necessary. In less clear-cut cases, the information must at least call into question the person's fitness for their position. The French and the Americans have seen that a constant, hypocritical, voyeuristic intrusion into the private lives of public figures is not in the public interest, even if it is *of* interest.

A general consensus like the French model is far more effective than any formal enforcement structure for continually working out and adapting the discriminations necessary, both between persons and between classes of information, if freedom of speech, investigative journalism, the right to know and the right to privacy are all to be met as far as possible. It can be done: such a consensus was effective in protecting the young Princes William and Harry after the death of their mother. Those honourable journalists who are capable of shame must surely want such a consensus.

3.4 Action

In effect, we have traded away our privacy in return for all the benefits offered by the internet. We have signed a blank cheque: we do not yet understand all the implications. This chapter has glanced briefly at some of them. There is also the information that is held on us without our knowledge or consent: we signed no cheque for that, so it was essentially stolen.

There seems to be nothing we can do to recover, protect or enlarge our privacy. We have no choice and therefore, in terms of the definition to be offered in chapter 4, in this respect no freedom. If we opt out of the internet (web and email) altogether, we suffer severe disadvantages; and even then, there is still the issue of our information stored on other systems. We might even become suspect as having something to hide, as pointed out by Eric Schmidt and Jared Cohen in their book *The New Digital Age* (Alfred A Knopf, 2013). That becomes even more likely if we try to protect our privacy by encrypting communications, installing extra security or using the darknet (see chapter 5). We have reached a stage when even to try to protect our privacy is likely to raise suspicion and to attract special attention from the security and law enforcement agencies.

But we are not powerless. We can use all our democratic options to require our elected representatives to devise institutions to hold to account all who have access to our information, whether government agencies, commercial companies or individuals. In chapter 6 on freedom and security, we shall look briefly at possible mechanisms for such accountability. In chapter 10, on freedom and democracy, we shall see that online democracy can be effective.

One way to do this is to support such campaigning organisations as Big Brother Watch and Liberty. They too are regarded with suspicion by the security agencies. Liberty suspects that its phone line is tapped. Until quite recently, that would have seemed ridiculously paranoid. Now, whether true or not, it seems all too plausible. But if to campaign for freedom is now seen as subversive, what have we come to?

If security agencies reply that they are screening for subversive elements infiltrating such organisations, not bona fide peace campaigners, then such intrusive blanket surveillance should require a judicial warrant, on the basis of reasonable suspicion, for each and every tap, and the awareness in confidence of the chief executive unless she too is a suspect.

As I sit at my computer typing this, I have no way of

knowing that even I am not on some list of suspects or 'potential extremists', and monitored. That is no longer ridiculous, and that fact alone should ring loud and urgent alarm bells.

Who is suspicious of lovers of freedom? Only dictators, actual or aspiring, and their henchmen.

But it might still be asked, what harm does state surveillance do me? Even if it means that others have power over me, does it infringe Mill's harm principle in practice? If such surveillance is essential to security, surely it is both necessary and beneficial? There are two separate issues here. One is whether Mill's view of freedom is adequate for the digital age: is the harm principle sufficient or does it need to be redefined? The other is the competing demands of security. The security issue will be addressed separately in chapter 6. We end Section 1 of this work, comprising chapters 1-4, by proposing a modified definition of a free country for our times.

4

Defining 'A Free Country' For the Digital Age

Freedom has a thousand charms to show,
that slaves, howe'er contented, never know.
William Cowper

The technology of the digital age has opened up possibilities that Mill could not have dreamed of. The interception of private communications was not an issue in his time. Technology leverages up hugely all the threats he wrote of, particularly the power of informal popular opinion (as through social networks), as well as that of excessive and intrusive government. It provides a huge range of new choices to the ordinary user, but also to criminals, companies and governments. We saw in chapter 1 that this constitutes anarchy, not freedom.

We have distinguished freedom from anarchy, from freedoms, from independence, from human rights and from rights in general. We have examined its relationship to privacy, and seen that taking and holding people's information does indeed diminish our freedom.

So we now need a definition of a free country that includes the right to privacy. As suggested in chapter 1, it should ideally define freedom not as the absence of constraint but as a positive, healthy condition, as a presence rather than an absence.

As a step towards such a working definition, a proposed form of words might be:

> A free country is one where every citizen has the greatest possible number of choices with responsibility for the consequences of choices made, without unaccepted risk of harm to others, and without being accountable to or watched by government or anyone else.

A few notes on this proposed definition:

1   It is intended to comprehend both freedom *from* and freedom *to*.
2   Since a choice made in ignorance of any relevant circumstances is not a true choice, the definition assumes *informed* choice.
3   We saw in chapter 1 that responsibility under the law is what differentiates freedom from anarchy, so it must be a part of the definition of freedom, and not a mere corollary.
4   The rule of law is not a part of the definition of freedom but an antecedent condition of it. Its effect is incorporated in the definition as responsibility.
5   It has been suggested that the aggregate of available choices is not a comprehensive definition of freedom in all circumstances. The example given is of a trusted slave who may have many more choices than a person who is free but very poor. However, to the extent that the slave's options are subject to the consent of his owner, they are not free choices. This remains the structural and legal reality however permissive or tolerant a particular owner

may be. For purposes of our enquiry into the profile of a free country, it is freedom under the law, or 'normative' freedom, that concerns us, not physical freedom. (A freedom-loving people will *also* want to increase physical options for as many citizens as possible, and we shall see in chapter 14 on freedom, literacy and development that normative and physical freedom can in some circumstances be inseparable.)

6   The range of choices available to the least free citizens is the measure of a country's true freedom. In the instance above, the freedom of both the privileged slave and the poor freeman would be measured. There are formidable difficulties in measuring the freedom of individual citizens. There are problems of definition, weighting and classification. There is a literature in which rival formulas are proposed.* These tend to be complicated, and so far as I know have remained theoretical and not applied. Perhaps Liberty or someone else could devise a rough-and-ready measure that might not satisfy the theorists and the statisticians, but give a good idea of the freedom of the least free in different countries and at different times. Measuring our freedom should be a continuous monitoring process conducted both in Parliament and by independent bodies such as Liberty.

7   Some innocent activities involve the risk of harm to others, such as boxing or rugby football. This is seen as consistent with the harm principle because all participants have accepted the risk. *Unaccepted* risk is not consistent with the principle.

8   'Others' must include future generations. To consume

---

* The idea of measuring freedom is not new. For a very complicated formula for quantifying the overall freedom of an individual, see Kramer, M., *The Quality of Freedom*, Oxford University Press, 2003. This is a very substantial work of social and political philosophy defining freedom in such a way as to make it measurable. See also Carter, I., *The Measure of Freedom*, Oxford University Press, 1999.

the earth's resources so as to leave nothing for our grandchildren, as we are doing with ocean fisheries for one example, is not significantly different from seizing them from our contemporaries – which we are also arguably doing. That is clearly anarchy, not freedom.

With this proposed definition of a free country in mind, we now examine the functions of law in a free country, the constitutional and legal structures necessary to ensure actual, enforceable, experienced freedom for every citizen, and the current position in the UK. We will then apply it to a range of issues.

The identity of an individual is essentially a function of her choices, rather than the discovery of an immutable attribute.
Amartya Sen, *The Argumentative Indian*
Allen Lane, 2005

Section 2

Constitutional Conditions of Freedom

5

Freedom, Law and Constitution: How Are We Doing?

The end of law is not to abolish or restrain, but to preserve and enlarge freedom.
John Locke, 1689

Sections 5.1 and 5.2 are intended to provide a very condensed introduction to the constitutional conditions necessary for freedom, for those without a background in law. Those with that knowledge may wish to skip to Section 5.3.

5.1 The functions of law in a free country

We have seen that anarchy tends to destroy freedom rather than enhance it, so we arrive at the central paradox: there can only be real freedom under the rule of law. But not all law protects freedom: bad law diminishes it. So what are the functions of law in a society which holds the freedom of the individual as a primary value?

We have only to formulate the question in this way to arrive at a preliminary answer: the law in a free country exists to protect and enlarge the freedom of the individual, and to

73

balance the freedom of each individual against that of others. We have seen that that will include ensuring that citizens take full responsibility for the consequences of their choices, both when those consequences are favourable and when they are adverse. In order to protect the freedom of citizens to go about their business without hindrance or fear, the law will maintain public order and security. As a part of balancing the freedoms of individuals, it will provide structures for conflict resolution, such as the civil courts. This view of the functions of law is the essence of Magna Carta's legacy.

By contrast, an absolute ruler is apt to see the law as a means of social control. Even kings, princes and presidents who have started out with altruistic ideals have often had to compromise them and been progressively corrupted by power. So we have to enquire what constitutional and legal structures are necessary for the law to fulfil its true function of protecting the freedom of each citizen. Then we will run a health check on the state and use of those structures in the UK today, with sidelong glances at the USA for comparison.

Our focus here is on constitutional structures and social and political freedom, but we might note in passing that something like absolute power can be experienced in the smaller structures of everyday life. A head teacher can make or break the professional prospects of any teacher on the staff. Charity trustees are accountable to no one, unlike company directors who are (at least in theory) accountable to shareholders. Since a charity has no shareholders, the trustees (who are usually also the directors) are not open to scrutiny unless they commit a criminal offence. These examples of near-absolute power on a local scale demonstrate the need for constitutional safeguards in the life of the nation.

5.2 Constitutional structures necessary to protect freedom: the theory

In the eighteenth century, the French thinker Montesquieu realised that citizens could only be truly free, independently of the whim of an all-powerful individual or clique, if a constitution existed which divided the powers of the state and allocated them to different institutions which were then set to keep a check on each other. The three powers of the state are the legislature to make the laws, the judiciary to interpret and apply the laws, and the executive to carry out and enforce the laws.

The theory requires that no individual should be involved in more than one of those three powers. A judge cannot be an MP; a police officer cannot also be a judge. A system of checks and balances between the three arms of the state is designed to prevent the accumulation of power in any one person, group or institution. Parliament, however, always remains sovereign.

Because the executive has the physical means to seize power, it is particularly important that the legislature and the judiciary should superintend and monitor it continuously to ensure it does not exceed the powers delegated to it. The judges must be protected from political influence. Only when the three powers are insulated from each other, with no person involved in more than one, can the checks and balances between them effectively protect the freedom of the citizen. Table 5.1 should make the theory clear. It applies to any constitution: minimal illustrations from those of the UK and the USA are given.

Great Britain has never had a written constitution, but its legal institutions have traditionally been framed on the basis of the separation of powers for the protection of the freedom of the individual. That freedom has always been a primary value, even – or especially – in wartime, but it has not always

75

Table 5.1 The separation of powers

The Powers and their functions	Who discharges these functions?	
	UK	**USA**
1 Legislature to make laws	Parliament (primary legislation); Delegated bodies, e.g. government departments, local councils. (secondary legislation)	Congress State legislatures Secondary legislation
2 Judiciary to interpret and apply the laws	Judges, courts	Judges, courts
3 Executive to carry out and enforce the law; administration	Police, armed forces, security services, the Civil Service; local government staff	Federal and state police, armed forces, security services, administration staff

applied to *all* citizens. It is still less than a century since women gained the right to vote in elections. Any concept of justice requires that freedom under the law is distributed equally among all citizens.

5.3 How far does present practice enact the theory and protect freedom?

A health check shows that the practice is not always as tidy as the theory. The USA was the first country to enact a written constitution that gave formal expression to the separation of powers, yet federal judges including those of the Supreme Court are appointed by the president, who is a party politician and the head of the executive. The Senate has a veto, but the initial choice is the president's. Such appointments are accepted as a means by which the president can 'colour' judicial decisions to match his political persuasion and other views. This clearly violates the separation of powers.

5.3.1 How it works in the UK: changing the constitution

The UK's unwritten constitution has also contained anomalies. In the Middle Ages, the Lord Chancellor was a very powerful official close to the king, virtually governing the country in his name. In later centuries, he acted as chairman of the House of Lords (which itself breached the separation of powers being both a part of the legislature and the final court of appeal), and as head of the judiciary, including appointing judges. He was not only involved in both the legislature and the judicature: he held commanding positions in both. In the curiously pragmatic way often characteristic of English legal institutions, this arrangement served reasonably well for some centuries. Successive Lord Chancellors generally observed the conventions of the unwritten constitution, including the separation of powers.

In more recent times, the Lord Chancellor was also given a seat in the Cabinet, giving him a presence in the executive. He then had a powerful position in all three functions of state. This was clearly anomalous. Its constitutional impropriety could no longer be overlooked when Lord Irvine of Lairg as Lord Chancellor sat in the House of Lords as a judge in the case of *Carmichael* v. *National Power plc* [1999]. The same person could not be a Cabinet minister and a judge. Questions also arose about whether such constitutional arrangements might fall foul of the ECHR. It was time to restore the separation of powers. But how?

If you were going to change a country's constitution, abolishing or changing arrangements that had stood for centuries, you would expect at the very least a royal commission including senior judges, academics and other experts, with wide terms of reference, to consult and deliberate before offering its recommendations to Parliament. Instead, late on Thursday 12 June 2003, Tony Blair as prime minister announced at a press conference that the post of

Lord Chancellor was to be abolished, that the functions of the Judicial Committee of the House of Lords (the final court of appeal) were to be transferred to a new Supreme Court, and that some of the functions of the Lord Chancellor and of the Home Office were to be transferred to a new secretary of state for constitutional affairs with a seat in the Cabinet. He then appointed his old friend Lord Falconer to be that secretary of state.

Blair had consulted no one. The Cabinet had met that morning but knew nothing of what was coming, because Lord Irvine, an old friend of Blair's, was present and his job was about to be abolished. Senior civil servants had not been consulted. The changes bore all the signs of haste: they had been discussed by a small inner circle for just 10 days. They had clearly not been thought through, and there was widespread consternation. The morning after the announcement, it was realised that the House of Lords could not sit without a Lord Chancellor, so the office was hastily re-created so that Lord Falconer could officiate. It then became clear that to abolish the post of Lord Chancellor would require an Act of Parliament.

It was certainly right to seek to re-establish the separation of powers, but there are two serious questions to be asked: did the proposed reforms achieve this end? And how constitutional was the process of change used by Blair?

The effectiveness seems doubtful. The three powers were indeed separated. The House of Lords was to choose its own chairman; the new Supreme Court was seen to be entirely separate from the legislature (unlike the old Judicial Committee of the House of Lords); judges were to be chosen by a new Judicial Appointments Commission (JAC). However, the secretary of state for constitutional affairs became in 2007 the Minister for Justice (still bizarrely combined with the title of Lord Chancellor), a party politician with a senior position in the Cabinet, who could reject the choices of the JAC (he would then have to supply a written explanation to the JAC). The minister is a serving MP, a member of both the legislature and the executive, and is involved in the appointment of judges and the administration of the courts: just like the former Lord Chancellor! As a result of the changes, the executive has more power, not less, over the administration of justice. Because the minister is a career politician sitting in the House of Commons, rather than a senior legal official in the House of Lords, he is appointed and directed by the prime minister. The very idea of a Ministry of Justice has an uncomfortably Orwellian ring to it.

As for Blair's process of simply announcing major constitutional changes by fiat and press conference, it is alarming that a prime minister could even think in those terms. As Professor Sir John Baker, the foremost authority on Magna Carta and mediaeval legal manuscripts, has observed, it is a disadvantage of the UK's unwritten constitution that it has no provision or procedure for changing or amending it (as the American constitution has), so it is open to creeping change without scrutiny or safeguards. (Personal conversation*) Blair was in his third term as prime minister, and had thus long had something close to absolute power. With an overwhelming majority in the House of Commons he virtually controlled the legislature, and through the Cabinet he controlled the executive. He has a legal background and claims knowledge of jurisprudence. His action shows all too clearly the necessity for robust checks and balances.

5.3.2 The roles of the prime minister and the Cabinet

The prime minister, then, has immense power in the legislature, especially when one party has an overwhelming

---

* For further material, type 'Professor Sir John Baker' into your search engine and select his Maccabean Lecture of 24 November 2009. See also under 'Miscellaneous' there a lecture on 'The Constitutional Revolution'.

majority in the House of Commons, as was the case with both Margaret Thatcher and Tony Blair. It is essential, if voters are to have a choice, that the opposition is a viable alternative government in waiting. If the opposition is unelectable, we have in effect a one-party state. Democracy is then undermined and freedom is threatened. Yet Margaret Thatcher could even boast of TINA: There Is No Alternative. She was clearly not too concerned about constitutional limits to her power.

The prime minister can even pack the House of Lords with her placemen, giving her control of the legislature as well as of the executive.

The Cabinet itself is a further constitutional anomaly. Chaired by the prime minister, it consists of his own chosen appointed ministers who head the various departments of government, that is, the executive; yet its members are also members of the legislature. Perhaps government departments should be headed by professional managers such as successful business figures, or the present permanent secretaries, accountable directly to Parliament through select committees and to a board chaired by the prime minister. Neither the managers nor the board should be MPs, but agree on recruitment to implement the election manifesto of the party in power. The board might include non-political figures such as successful people in various sectors of the country's life, but must in any case be politically balanced, perhaps in proportion to each party's share of the total vote in the most recent general election, with a proportion of members who are not politically aligned. Quite apart from the need to ensure the separation of powers, elected politicians do not necessarily make good managers.

However, one potential disadvantage of professionalising government in this way might be the need to provide alternative scope and incentives for able and ambitious politicians. If we want to attract the most able into government, responsibility and scope are essential. Membership of the prime minister's board and, for MPs, of select committees with enhanced powers might be a part of the answer.

There is also the surprisingly controversial issue of whether the head of the executive – the president in the USA, the prime minister in the UK – should be empowered to take the nation to war without a specific democratic mandate, as Blair did in Iraq. That episode is the subject of the Chilcot Report, being prepared by the official inquiry into the UK's involvement. It has been delayed for four years, allegedly by Blair's refusal to publish 25 of his notes to President Bush and more than 130 records of conversations between either Tony Blair or Gordon Brown and President Bush. (Sources: letter from Sir John Chilcot to the Prime Minister of 4/11/13, on The Iraq Inquiry website; *The Times*, 19/5/14, quoting the *Mail on Sunday* of 18/5/14). Blair rejects this allegation.

Both Thatcher and Blair took opportunities to centralise power. One person having control of both the legislature and the executive contradicts the separation of powers. It seems that Mr Blair, an elected politician at the time, still does not regard himself as accountable to those who elected him, or to those affected by his decisions relating to the invasion of Iraq.

5.3.3 Is the executive effectively accountable to Parliament?

One test of the separation of powers is the extent to which the executive is effectively accountable to Parliament. The House of Commons can summon a minister or a secretary of state to the House to answer questions, but this procedure does not in practice provide an opportunity to scrutinise the executive's actions systematically. Since 1979 the House of Commons has appointed a select committee to monitor each department of government. They can collect evidence, appoint specialist advisers, and require powerful people to appear before them and answer searching questions. This makes good copy and television. A select committee can report to the House, but the government is not bound to implement the committee's report and recommendations. The select committees can therefore seem toothless. Their influence can be considerable, but it is moral, not legal.

The composition of the select committees also undermines confidence. The chairpersons have, since 2010, been elected by the House as a whole, but the other members are party appointees. The Intelligence and Security Committee, tasked to review the surveillance activities of GCHQ following the Snowden revelations, is chaired by Sir Malcolm Rifkind, even though as foreign secretary he was previously responsible for the organisation he is now reviewing. The other members of this committee, unlike the members of other committees, are appointed by the prime minister, and are all connected with the security establishment.

On 7 November 2013, the Intelligence and Security Committee held an unprecedented open session in which the heads of GCHQ, MI5 and MI6 all appeared to answer questions. It looked like an impressive example of the elected legislature calling the executive to account. But it emerged in *The Sunday Times* of 17 November 2013 that it was almost entirely scripted. The service heads only agreed to appear after a year of negotiations, in which the areas of questioning were agreed, with how much time would be allotted to each area, and what the first question in each area would be. Only a third of the time would be allocated to the Snowden revelations. The Cabinet Office insists that the event was 'not scripted', but the chiefs would have little difficulty in guessing the questions that would follow the first in each area. The outcome of the Committee's investigations seemed entirely predictable.

What are we seeing here? We are seeing nothing less than a collusion between the legislature and the executive to deceive the public into thinking that the executive is under democratic control, whereas the security chiefs were apparently allowed virtually to dictate the terms on which they would appear. In the words of one Conservative MP, 'Evidently the whole thing was a total pantomime.'

5.3.4 The security services

We looked in chapter 3 at the implications of universal surveillance for privacy and therefore freedom, and in chapter 6 we shall look at the competing claims of security and privacy. Here we note the constitutional implications. No less an authority than Sir Tim Berners-Lee, who made the internet possible by devising the hypertext transfer protocol, has come out strongly in support of Edward Snowden, the American whistle-blower, slating the security authorities of the USA and the UK. Among other things, he was reported in the BBC and other news of 7 November 2013 as saying that 'the system of checks and balances' to oversee GCHQ and its US counterpart the National Security Agency 'had failed'. In using the phrase *checks and balances*, he is referring explicitly to the separation of powers. He is stating that the security agencies in both countries are out of control. This is clearly true. It implies an immediate constitutional crisis and a direct threat to our freedom, yet the country's response so far has been comatose.

The populations of both countries are left to assume that the security agencies acted first and thought about constitutional propriety afterwards, if at all. We shall ask in chapter 6 what emergency could justify such actions in a free country.

5.3.5 The police

It is not only the security services, but also the police and the administration – both sectors of the executive arm of the state – that now threaten our freedom.

For decades it has been obvious that many police officers have scant regard for truth or for justice. From covering up their own wrongdoing, as at Hillsborough in 1989, to 'verballing' suspects, it has become an inescapable conclusion that many police officers see themselves as above the law. ('Verballing' is fabricating statements and attributing them falsely to people being questioned.) John Bromley-Davenport QC, a barrister with long experience, says that the practice is 'endemic in every force in the land and many judges [are] blind to the obvious dishonesty of police officers'. Over six years, the Metropolitan Police alone paid out £8.9 million to settle complaints.

The Sunday Times reported on 16 November 2014: 'In just nine months, between December 2013 and August this year, 173 constables, 23 sergeants, nine inspectors and three chief inspectors were dismissed for misconduct or resigned or retired before proceedings could be brought. Misconduct by the officers included eight instances of assault while on duty, 16 cases of theft and three cases involving child sex offences'.

Police self-regulation has clearly failed to maintain public confidence. Sir Hugh Orde, the president of the Association of Chief Police Officers, has said we need 'a completely independent police investigation system – I think it is critical'. (Source for this and the previous paragraph: David Leppard in *The Sunday Times*, 20/10/13).

Doubtless there are honest individuals, but they can find it difficult or impossible to prevail in a corrupt culture, and may pay a heavy price in career prospects. Some have left the force, leaving the corrupt in the ascendancy in some places. Polls show that many people still do trust the police, but there is a growing popular perception that the 'good cops' no longer characterise the force as they once did, at least in parts of the cities, where most people live. It is no longer a case of 'a few rotten apples': much of the barrel is now suspect.

Perhaps the new publicly elected police commissioners

will be able at last to make the police publicly accountable in a way that the Independent Police Complaints Commission has not. The experiment should be given time to bed in and given every support and every chance of success, but monitored continually and publicly on its record. It should be replaced promptly if it too proves ineffective.

Meanwhile, if the facts are as they appear, the legislature and the judiciary have to bring the police to heel and enforce their subordination to the law. That will take more courage and determination than was shown by the Intelligence and Security Committee. An excellent start was made by Theresa May in her speech as home secretary at the Police Federation conference on 21 May 2014. The Federation has shown alarming lack of transparency and accountability for some time; it has appeared to be the epicentre of the rot in the barrel. Mrs May, unlike her predecessors, read out a long list of indictments, and made it clear that change was now inevitable. If the Federation did not accept the recommendations of the Normington Review on police reform, they would be imposed. Where previous home secretaries have been booed, she was heard in stunned silence. Members then voted to accept all 36 recommendations of the review.

The Home Secretary has since determined to ensure that police misconduct hearings will be held in public for the first time, that disciplinary panels will have the power to reduce the pensions and other benefits of senior officers found guilty of wrongdoing, and that whistle-blowers who expose corrupt colleagues will be protected. (Source: *The Sunday Times*, 16/11/14.) These are precisely the kind of reforms that are needed, although only a start. The real question raised is: why were these arrangements not made in the first place?

If politicians fail to enforce the rule of law in unmistakeable fashion, that will demonstrate that we are already living in a police state, where the police are above the law and habitually abuse their power. The longer these elements of the executive are out of control, the more consolidated their position will become, and the harder it will be to restore accountability. We are now at a watershed.

5.3.6 The administrative services

Less obvious is the growing and intrusive power of the administrative part of the executive, such as Cabinet ministers, the Civil Service and town halls. The problem here is different. It is not usually that national and local government officers are exceeding their powers, but rather that the powers delegated to them are far too widely drawn and open to abuse.

At the national level, government ministers, who hold powerful positions in both the legislature and the executive, have been given powers that properly belong to the courts. These include issuing warrants for surveillance, parole decisions in prisons and what amounts to arbitrary power in relation to immigration appeals.

At the local level, the powers delegated to administrators seem to fall into two groups. The first consists of powers of punishment being taken from the courts and given to officials, so that the safeguards of due court process are bypassed. This started with routine offences where the facts are not disputed, such as speeding and parking offences. 'On the spot' fines would, it was hoped, make the punishment immediate and so more effective and the process faster and cheaper than court procedures and delays. Administrative, as opposed to judicial, punishment has spread to many other 'offences', such as putting out the rubbish the day before collection, smoking in a van (on the grounds that it is a workplace), exhibiting a *disabled* car sticker upside down, or dropping two crisps in the gutter. These are actual examples given by Raab (pp. 73-75).

The increasing use by local councils of closed-circuit

television (CCTV) cameras, both fixed and in cars, to catch parking offenders was the subject of a report by Big Brother Watch in April 2014. In response, Brandon Lewis MP, minister for local government, said: 'I welcome this exposé by Big Brother Watch. It is clear that CCTV is being used to raise money in industrial volumes for town halls, breaking the constitutional principle that fines should not be used as a source of revenue.' With respect to the minister, a far more fundamental constitutional principle being broken here is punishment increasingly being removed from the courts and handed to the administrative part of the executive. This breaches the separation of powers by giving judicial powers and functions to politically appointed officials, and denies the accused the safeguards of due process.

The officials who find themselves in a quasi-judicial role do not necessarily have any legal training, but they are clearly under pressure to raise revenue. When revenue-raising becomes the purpose of law enforcement, it is no longer a function of justice, but still operates with the weight of legal sanction. This causes widespread cynicism and brings the rule of law itself into disrepute. If constitutional authorities themselves undermine the rule of law, where might this lead?

There is a right of appeal to the courts, but if the appeal is lost the appellant may be faced with a much higher fine or even imprisonment. There is evidence that many who receive a spot fine and feel it to be unjustified still pay the fine because they cannot afford the risk of an adverse outcome of an appeal.

There are arguments to be made for the original use by police and traffic wardens of spot fines in routine cases where the facts are not in dispute, such as speeding and parking fines, but extending such powers widely to local councils was surely a mistake. If due process is seen to be slow and expensive, then we must make it fast and cheap –

and keep punishment where it belongs, as a part of justice administered by the courts.

The other group of administrative threats to freedom includes actions other than punishment by police and officials, such as powers of interception. The RIPA 2000, as we saw in chapter 3, allowed no less than 514,608 interceptions and authorisations in 2013 alone. The commissioner for interception has reported that, of these, most were by police and other law enforcement agencies; the rest were by local authorities using powers delegated to them under the Act. Some 132 local authorities reported using their powers in 2013, with Birmingham City Council, and Bromley and Enfield London Borough Councils, topping the table with 87 each. Even that does not tell anything like the full story: local authorities can completely bypass RIPA *and judicial oversight* when using their powers on benefits and housing fraud. (Source: LocalGov.co.uk, 9/4/14, my italics).

Similarly, there are delegated powers of entry into our homes or other premises. Until some were withdrawn by the Protection of Freedoms Act 2012 (PFA), there were no less than 1,400 powers of entry under primary and secondary legislation. More on this Act later.

Appeals under a considerable amount of primary and secondary legislation lie not to a court of law but to an administrative tribunal. There is a whole hierarchy of appeal tribunals collectively called The General Regulatory Chamber. This is a part of the new Ministry of Justice, and is therefore a part of the executive. Its structure mimics that of the courts, also administered by the Ministry of Justice, and the tribunals assume judicial functions. They have developed their own procedures, and they are doubtless meticulously fair, but they are independent of the due process of the courts. An independent judiciary can keep a check on abuses of power. Government-appointed tribunals lack that independence. Removing more and more causes from the courts to tribunals is a direct threat to an independent judiciary, and therefore to our freedom.

It is perhaps arguable that the courts have to some extent brought this on themselves. In the Middle Ages, the common law courts became very rigid, and limited in their ability to adapt to social change. An alternative and more flexible system of law called equity grew up alongside the common law, with its own court, that of Chancery, to offer justice in new situations which the common law courts failed to address. The administrative tribunals today look very much like a parallel judicial system. Has it grown up in part because the courts can be characterised, rightly or wrongly, as rigid, slow and expensive? It is essential to our freedom that the administration of justice remains in the hands of a truly independent judiciary, and therefore that the courts reinvent themselves where necessary to be seen as accessible, cheap, quick and adaptable in their administration. Some excellent starts have been made, such as the small claims divisions of the county courts, but more needs to be done, and done urgently, to deprive the executive of excuses to remove more and more causes into its own domain.

Some consider that the ever-expanding scope of the administrative arm of the state, and of administrative law, constitutes the most insidious threat of all to our freedom. Professor Hayek said in a lecture as far back as 1955: '... it is in the technical discussion concerning administrative law that the fate of our liberty is being decided' (Cit. Leoni, OLL).

5.3.7 What protects our freedom now?

So has the separation of powers broken down? Apart from citizen groups like Big Brother Watch and Liberty, our freedom is now constitutionally defended by only two remaining bulwarks, an independent judiciary and a free press. It is highly significant that both are under attack.

i The judiciary

For centuries, the High Court and its predecessors, especially the Queen's Bench Division, have vigilantly protected the freedom of the individual citizen, using a number of *prerogative writs*. These are commands from the court to someone requiring them to do, or to refrain from doing, some action to enforce the law. The main means of protecting freedom is the ancient writ of habeas corpus, which requires someone believed to be holding a citizen against her will to produce that person in court and to justify the detention. It has traditionally been regarded, with the right to trial by jury, as one of the very greatest protections of the freedom of the individual.

Winston Churchill will always be regarded as one of the great protectors of the English tradition of freedom. In 1943, at the height of the war, he wrote of

> ...the great privilege of habeas corpus, and of trial by jury, which are the supreme protection invented by the English people for ordinary people against the state ... The power of the Executive to cast a man into prison without formulating any charge known to the law and particularly to deny him the judgement of his peers – is, in the highest degree, odious and is the foundation of all totalitarian governments...
>
> (Cit. Raab, p. 31)

Anyone with any concern for freedom will recognise the vital, even pivotal, role of habeas corpus. Yet, having survived for centuries, habeas corpus has been progressively weakened in recent years, especially by the Prevention of Terrorism Act 2005 (PTA), to the point where it is seldom used. More and more powers of detention and release have been transferred from the courts to the home secretary.

To some extent, the courts have compensated by developing judicial review. This is a new term for the old prerogative writs, which have always been the citizen's only way of challenging the abuse of power, whether by the state or by others. Yet the government is contemplating curtailing judicial review on the specious grounds of economy and reducing delays, as if it was an optional and dispensable extra. The government states that judicial review has expanded greatly, as if that were a reason to limit it: if true, it shows that it is meeting a need and is clearly a reason to protect it. The Joint Committee on Human Rights (JCHR), a committee of both Houses of Parliament and all major parties, has criticised this move, dismissing the government's grounds as lacking evidence.

The Public Law Project, an independent and recognised authority on public law, produced in February 2014 a briefing paper in which it says that the reforms proposed in Part 4 of the current Criminal Justice and Courts Bill will not have the effects claimed for them, but that, even as amended, the legislation will have the effect of limiting people's access to the courts, and 'will suppress legitimate challenge and insulate unlawful executive action from judicial scrutiny ... Parliament must be aware that the proposals threaten to undermine our constitution and destabilise our democracy'. Strong words. See the Public Law Project website for more detail.

Perhaps more significant even than both of these alarm calls, Lord Neuberger, president of the Supreme Court, is so concerned that he has spoken out publicly on this issue. I quote fully from the *Telegraph* of 15 October 2013:

Lord Neuberger, president of the Supreme Court, said the courts have an important function to protect the public from the 'abuses' of public authorities by allowing people to seek a review of decisions. He acknowledged the Government was looking at ways of saving money and delays in the system, but warned changes must be carefully considered 'because of the importance of maintaining judicial review'.

'With the ever-increasing power of Government, which now commands almost half the country's gross domestic product, this function of calling the executive to account could not be more important. I am not suggesting that we have a dysfunctional or ill-intentioned executive, but the more power that a government has, the more likely it is that there will be abuses and excesses which result in injustice to citizens, and the more important it is for the rule of law that such abuses and excesses can be brought before an impartial and experienced judge who can deal with them openly, dispassionately and fairly.'

Lord Neuberger made his comments as he delivered the annual Tom Sargant Memorial Lecture.

When the most senior judge in the country speaks out in these terms, we should be seriously concerned, because any freedom-loving government would support, not seek to erode, judicial review. But we can also be reassured and grateful that we still have judges who are prepared to challenge government to protect our freedom.

When the executive really takes over, even the courts may be ignored. In the archive of the *Washington Post* of 15 August 2013, we can read the only known account, from the 12 October 2011 edition of *SSO News*, the internal newsletter of the National Security Agency, of a decision by the Foreign Intelligence Surveillance Court that the NSA was using illegal methods in collecting the private communications of US citizens. The case does not appear in the official records, and the judgement seems to have had no noticeable effect on the activities of the NSA, which has continued to expand. No wonder Lord Neuberger is worried.

ii A free press

As an executive increases its power, it can eventually ignore not only the courts but the press. If necessary it can introduce covert or overt censorship, or close down the more independent and vigilant media.

The attack on press freedom arises from outrage at apparently widespread abuses by the press, such as the Milly Dowler case. This is expressed through a very vociferous pressure group called Hacked Off, which presses for legal curbs on press freedom and therefore on the freedom of speech. The Leveson Review was an attempt at a compromise, with freedom as the norm but with a statutory control of media as a last resort. The outcome is still unclear, with *The Guardian*, the *The Independent* and *The Financial Times* currently refusing to sign up to the proposed structure. The details are available on several websites.

We explored this issue in its relation to privacy in chapter 3. As we noted there, the press largely brought this on itself by its failure to control its own rogue elements, but the fact remains, as press bodies stridently remind us, that freedom depends on media that are free to investigate abuses proactively (whereas the courts are necessarily reactive). As George Orwell put it: 'If liberty means anything at all, it means the right to tell people what they do not want to hear.' (Original preface to *Animal Farm*; as published in *George Orwell: Some Materials for a Bibliography* (1953) by Ian R. Willison.)

As we also saw in chapter 3, a more insidious threat to an investigative press lies in the internet. As more people go online to get their news, newspaper circulations fall, and so do advertising revenues. Investigative reporting is expensive. If it gets to a stage where newspapers, online and offline, can no longer afford it, we may lose one of the last two protections of our freedom.

5.4 The laws in a free country

If law exists in a free country to ensure and extend the freedom of the individual, constitutional law is just the starting point. The effective separation of powers is necessary but not sufficient for ensuring the freedom of the individual. The laws themselves must protect freedom. We saw in chapter 1, in considering the rule of law, that there can be bad law: both Stalin and Hitler operated within the rule of (bad) law. We shall look further at the abuse of the legislative process in chapter 7, and briefly at the quandary of the law-abiding citizen faced by bad law in chapter 15.

As we saw earlier, the first function of law and the first duty of any government is to protect the people. This includes defence, effective border control and the maintenance of public order. The apparent tension between freedom and security will be considered in chapter 6.

The PFA 2012 addresses a series of discrete freedoms. It rectifies one clear abuse by the executive: the retention on police databases of the biometric data (DNA and fingerprints) of innocent people. These have now been deleted, and the DNA of murderers and rapists added. Other issues addressed include modifying stop and search powers, and reducing the maximum period of detention without charge from 21 to 14 days; yet another commissioner, this time for surveillance cameras; wheel-clamping on private land, and other issues. Credit where credit is due: the Act rectifies some abuses and protects certain freedoms, but this merely nibbles at the edges of freedom as we have defined it. A modern Magna Carta it is not.

The maintenance of public order has sometimes been abused as a pretext and a method for seizing power, especially in times of social insecurity. Our view of the functions of law in a free country becomes particularly relevant at this point: the purpose of public order law is precisely the same as that of all law, namely to protect the freedom of individuals to go about their lawful business without hindrance or being put in fear. This is the essence of Magna Carta and of the ancient concept of The King's Peace, and the only legitimate function of public order law. Laws that unnecessarily restrict rather than protect the individual's freedom would be seen as unconstitutional in a free country, and struck down by a constitutional court empowered to do so, as suggested in chapter 16.

The PTA 2005 would receive special scrutiny. This gives the home secretary power to imprison indefinitely anyone even suspected, not convicted, of terrorist activity. Apart from issues of detention without trial and therefore without a jury, the Act effectively transgresses the separation of powers and disables the writ of habeas corpus, as we noted earlier. It gives a member of the executive, who is also an MP, what is clearly a judicial function.

5.5 Summary

What does our health check show? It shows a prime minister with virtually unchecked power across the legislature and the executive, power which can eventually create delusions of being above the law and the constitution; a Cabinet, chosen and chaired by the prime minister which has power in all three arms of the state; security and police services behaving as if they were above the law and evading accountability; and an administration which, at both national and local levels, increasingly takes judicial powers away from independent courts and due process. All this is happening in a democracy. We have only ourselves to blame if we allow this state of affairs to continue or to increase.

*   *   *

95

One mark of a free country is the extent to which legislators, constantly vigilant for the individual's freedom, seek to limit it as little as possible, and therefore make as few laws as possible. In recent times, the trend has been the opposite. Governments have made new laws on an epic scale, creating many new offences. We shall look briefly at this in chapter 7 on 'the 'legislative itch'. Meanwhile, we turn now to the pressing and topical issue of the tension between our need for security and the value we put on our freedom.

Section 3

Some Applications and Implications

6

Freedom and Security

In a crisis it is easier to act than to think.
Hannah Arendt

In chapter 3 on freedom and privacy, we looked at the surveillance of all internet traffic that is carried out by governments in the name of security. We saw that it violates the privacy and therefore the freedom of all users of the internet, and even of non-users whose information is stored in computers that are connected to the internet. In this chapter we examine the justifications we are offered for this violation. Is it really necessary for our security? Is it excessive? Is it effective?

6.1 When can universal surveillance be justified?

In times of danger, such as war or pandemic, freedom has to be severely limited. Peacetime parameters have to be set aside. When security is at risk, it trumps freedom every time.

But herein also lie dangers. Governments may be tempted to exaggerate, or even create or invent, a threat as a pretext for imposing martial law or other controls which would not

99

otherwise be acceptable. This can be a very tempting option for a government that is failing and needs a diversion, or an excuse to raise taxes. Many agendas can be hidden behind a scary security scenario.

A further temptation arises from the mere existence of the technical means of surveillance and control. As soon as something becomes possible, it seems we have to do it. We do because we can. And if we do not do it, someone else will.

The first question, then, is always: how real is the danger? Following 9/11, the July bombings in London and other atrocities elsewhere, there is no doubt about the jihadist threat. Since many radicalised jihadists live among peaceable Muslims and among the indigenous population, intelligence-gathering is essential to public security. Every peace-loving citizen will want all possible means to be used to minimise and defeat the threat.

Does this require vetting *all* communication on the internet? Perhaps it does, since aggressors and other criminals will seek to communicate in undetectable ways, and will also have access to the necessary expertise. The darknet, where complete anonymity is made possible, originally created by the American military to protect its communications, is also used by terrorist, criminal and paedophile networks. We saw in chapter 5 that Sir Tim Berners-Lee sees the security agencies as out of control. He has also said: 'Sometimes people do have to spy on the internet for law enforcement. We have to figure out how to balance that against rights.' (Source: *The Times*, 19/5/14). That we have not yet achieved this balance is clear from a report in *The Independent* for 17 June 2014. To quote in full:

In the first detailed defence of the UK's surveillance policies since the Snowden revelations, Charles Farr, the director general of the Office for Security and Counter-Terrorism, has said that the surveillance of ... popular

100

sites is legal because their US origin means they count as 'external communications'.

In a 48-page statement issued in response to a legal challenge brought by Privacy International, Liberty, Amnesty International and seven other national civil liberties groups, Farr admits that the government allows the interception of a massive range of online activities without a warrant.

It was previously thought that the interception of communications within the country was covered by section 8(1) of the Regulation of Investigatory Powers Act 2000 (RIPA), with warrants granted when law enforcement suspected the individual in question of illegal activity.

However, by defining these web services as 'external communications', they fall under the general warrants of section 8(4) of RIPA. This means that a range of activities – from emails to Facebook messages to Google searches – can all be intercepted even when the police have no grounds to suspect the individuals of wrongdoing.

Farr argues that the convoluted paths that data can take across the internet justify an indiscriminate approach to data collection: 'The only practical way in which the government can ensure that it is able to obtain at least a fraction of the type of communication in which it is interested is to provide for the interception of a large volume of communication.'

Referring to the concern that analysts would therefore be able to read the private communications of law abiding citizens, Farr said: 'The analyst, being only human and having a job to do, will have forgotten (if he or she ever took it in) what the irrelevant communication contained.'

Eric King, deputy director of Privacy International, said: 'The suggestion that violations of the right to privacy are meaningless if the violator subsequently forgets about it not only offends the fundamental, inalienable nature of human rights, but patronises the British people, who will not accept such a meagre excuse for the loss of their civil liberties.'

This information would not have been made public without the challenge of the independent organisations named.

Meanwhile, in the USA the NSA programme has allowed the government to collect a greater range of foreign intelligence 'quickly and effectively', the Privacy and Civil Liberties Oversight Board said in a report released on 2 July 2014. It added, however, that certain aspects of the programme raise questions about whether its impact on US persons pushes it over the edge into 'constitutional unreasonableness'. The watchdog said it was concerned about the incidental collection of US persons' communications, and the use of queries to search the information collected under the programme for the communications of specific US persons.

The programme, part of the US Foreign Intelligence Surveillance Act (FISA), collects electronic communications, including telephone calls and emails, where the target is a non-US citizen located outside the USA.

So it is legal for the security agencies in each country to collect the communications of the other's citizens and then exchange the information. Should we accept assurances that the security agencies act entirely within the law? They may (at times) observe the letter of the law while circumventing its purpose.

And even that is not enough: they survey their own citizens also, apparently regardless of constitutional or legal niceties.

To justify this, the threat must be real, deadly and imminent. Theresa May, the home secretary, says there are at least two such threats: dangerous criminals, and trained and hardened jihadists returning from the Syrian conflict. In *The Sunday Times* of 29 June 2014, she is reported as saying that, in London alone, Scotland Yard had had to drop 12 serious criminal investigations in three months because detectives were not allowed access to suspects' communications, and that 'up to' 300 jihadists had returned to the UK after fighting in Iraq and Syria. This does not explain why warrants could not be obtained, but there seems no reason to disbelieve her.

If this is the case, the powers must be given. Libertarians who try to resist under these circumstances would risk losing all credibility. Libertarians should instead insist on the principle that judicial (not ministerial) supervision and visible accountability must always be proportionate to the powers. If more powers are being requested, the structures for supervision and accountability must also be increased and equivalent, and be seen to be so. The emergency Data Retention and Investigation Powers Act 2014 (DRIPA) appears to meet these concerns, with a new Privacy and Civil Liberties Oversight Board (PCLOB) to scrutinise the impact of the law on privacy and civil liberties. The new law will automatically lapse at the end of 2016, giving the new government time to consider a wider review in the light of circumstances at that time.

This appears to be well balanced and it is important to acknowledge that, but we have heard such rhetoric before, especially when a government wants to rush a bill through Parliament, even for the best of reasons. The urgency is unconvincing and suspicious: the bill was proposed as a response to the Gonzalez judgement (see chapter 3), but that case was heard back in April 2014. Where was the urgency? Then to rush it through Parliament in three days without scrutiny or debate is to despise and destroy democracy.

Moreover, the Act is designed to compel internet service providers (ISPs) to retain information such as communications so as to be available to security agencies, and this is claimed to be necessary as a correction to the effects of the Gonzalez judgement. But that judgement does not give a complainant a right to have the material erased. All it requires is the deletion of the link from Google (or other search engine) to the material. That text remains as before on the original source, such as a newspaper's website. It can still be found there by searching for other terms in the text, or even by using Google.com rather than through a national website such as Google.co.uk. So even the claimed reason for the Act does not match the alleged threat, quite apart from the urgency. For an excellent explanation of this, with related material, see Cian Traynor's clear piece under the heading 'Netfix' in *The Irish Times* magazine section of 16 July 2014. The security services want both the link and the content.

Even if we accept that the intentions are good, implementation is always another matter. Actions that follow once a bill is law do not always match the rhetoric offered when the bill was being promoted. Libertarians will be performing a useful role by monitoring implementation, especially since the law was drafted and passed in such haste. For example, who will select the members of the PCLOB? How far will its scope extend? What powers will it have? To whom will the Board report? What authority will its findings have? How much will be made public? Above all, is this a judicial or an administrative body? We saw in chapter 5 that the steady encroachment of the executive on the functions of the judiciary is perhaps the most serious of all the threats to our freedom. It is encouraging that the Act reduces the number of agencies that can have legal access to communications. Three local police forces, several minor government departments, Royal Mail and the Charities Commission all lose access. (See www.UKauthority.com for more detail.) We might be surprised that such bodies were ever given access, but at least their removal indicates awareness in government of public concern about the imbalance against privacy. The crucial issue, however, is whether supervision at the national level is judicial, in the courts, or 'administrative', in the Home Office, which is a part of the executive. That would mean the Home Office minding its own, a clear conflict of interest.

Perhaps there is also a danger that public concern will be so fixated on the surveillance issue that the threat from administrative law is not noticed.

6.2 What protection does the law provide?

DRIPA does not supersede RIPA: it refines and extends it. So what protections do RIPA and DRIPA provide in the UK? The history is instructive. Together with the Justice and Security Act 2013 (JSA), they form a very complicated set of legislation, creating a series of overlapping agencies and officials. There is an intelligence services commissioner, who must be or have been a senior judge and is appointed and directed by the prime minister (the leader of both the legislature and the executive now directing a judicial function); but there is also an interception of communications commissioner. We have noted the Information Commissioner's Office. The Office for Security and Counter-Terrorism, mentioned above, is a police unit in the Home Office. In chapter 3, we noted the existence of the IPT, the only tribunal where a citizen can complain of a breach of privacy by the state. Again, membership, powers and functions are in the hands of the executive; proceedings are not necessarily open to the complainant, and there is no appeal to a court of law. Is the PCLOB to be added to this already ungainly structure? If so, how will it fit in?

Information on all these bodies is available on their various websites. Even so, it is not at all clear how these functions relate to each other. Information is ostensibly available, yet it is still virtually impossible for an ordinary citizen to find out her rights and safeguards from the official websites. Exploring the constitutional implications is out of the question without specialist knowledge.

The importance the government attaches to these safeguards is measured by the resources it makes available to them. On 27 June 2014, Big Brother Watch reported:

> The Intelligence Services Commissioner has released his annual report which highlights a high number of times individuals' privacy was breached due to a series of errors. However, with only 17% of warrants being checked by the Commissioner, serious questions have also been raised about how thorough his investigations can actually be.

> It is not unfair to suggest that at present the oversight by the Commissioner is weak and his accountability to Parliament and the public is almost non-existent. A part-time Commissioner with only one member of staff cannot reasonably provide adequate oversight of the use of intrusive surveillance powers. As the Home Affairs Select Committee recently pointed out, the Commissioner should be aiming to check at least 50% of warrants if the investigations are to be thorough.

> It is clear that the Government must urgently address the fact that the Commissioner clearly does not have enough resources to thoroughly carry out his investigations into the intelligence and security services.

The government, judging by its actions and its use of resources, does not appear to be serious about protecting the privacy of its citizens. The risk is that such structures, far from gaining public confidence, come to be seen as fig-leaves, cynical devices designed to give the false impression that freedom and privacy are protected, while the government's real agendas lie elsewhere.

What all these agencies and officials have in common is that they are all appointed and directed by, and accountable to, the executive arm of the state in the name of security. Is the executive using security as a pretext for expanding its power?

Secret courts and trials are one key issue:

The Justice and Security Act 2013 (JSA) originated in a consultative or green paper introduced by the then justice secretary, Kenneth Clarke, in 2011. This was an over-the-top affair, proposing to make secret procedures available in all types of civil proceedings, not just those cases involving national security, and even when the government itself was involved. It further proposed that the government should have the power to decide for itself whether to invoke the secret procedure, with only very limited review by the court. While the House of Lords duly removed these provisions during the passage of the bill through Parliament, the intentions of the government were pretty clear. A dangerously reactionary and repressive piece of legislation was to be introduced, ironically, under cover of improving oversight of the security and intelligence services.

The Law Society of England and Wales, representing solicitors, argued that the JSA infringed open justice and jeopardised the right to a fair trial based on equality of arms as an essential element of the rule of law. In the same vein, the barrister Michael Fordham commented: 'Secret trials undermine the principles of open justice and natural justice on which the rule of law is built.' The spread of secrecy allows 'the state authorities to become self-immunised from proper public scrutiny', he contended.

(Source: Rod Jones of OpenDemocracy. www.open democracy.net/opensecurity, where more information can be found)

These facts strongly suggest that there is indeed an assault on our liberty, and that the statutory protections are inadequate.

Power is addictive. The more we have, the more we want. That is why the separation of powers and constitutional checks and balances have evolved over the centuries. Such structures assume, as must we, that there are at least elements in the security agencies that will take any opportunity to extend their reach and their power. The executive arm of the state has always had to be watched vigilantly. The need for scrutiny and accountability is not new, but the technology of surveillance and IT has leveraged it massively. The possibilities for both good and ill are unprecedented. The need for *effective and visible* checks and balances has never been greater.

6.3 A security state?

The immediacy of the jihadist threat can obscure other dangers and allow us to be led into panicky, unbalanced responses. If a 'security state' becomes established, so that all citizens are scrutinised all the time, then our state is different in no significant way from that of the enemy. This would put peaceable Muslims in even more of a quandary than they already are, for it would deprive them of a major reason to support the state against terrorists.

Yet that Muslim majority's support is essential for defeating the tiny but violently destructive jihadist minority. On Saturday 21 June 2014, an estimated 5,000 young Muslim men gathered in Surrey to pledge loyalty to Britain in light of concerns over the popularity of ISIS and the alleged involvement of Britons. The three-day residential event was organised by the Ahmadiyya Muslim Youth Association (Amya) to foster bonds of brotherhood and affirm their pride in being British and Muslim. (Source: *The Guardian*, 22/6/14). Such responses must receive discreet but real recognition and support: the British public will be reassured, and suspicion directed not to all Muslims but only to the jihadist element. A blanket clampdown or surveillance could have the opposite effect, polarising the majority Muslim community.

We can extrapolate from the particular UK situation to a generalisation: if freedom is not preserved and valued even in the face of threats – especially then – we have already lost the conflict because we have lost the only thing worth fighting for: our freedom. The point was eloquently made by the renowned senior judge Lord Hoffman in 2004. In the security climate following 9/11, the UK government had sought derogation from Article 5(1) of the ECHR, guaranteeing personal freedom. He said:

> The real threat to the life of the nation, in the sense of a people living in accordance with its traditional laws and political values, comes not from terrorism but from laws such as these. That is the true measure of what terrorism may achieve. (*A v Secretary of State for the Home Department* [2004] UKHL 56)

So it is not a straight zero-sum trade-off between freedom and security, not that more of one means less of the other. We have to have both as far as possible. If it is once accepted that the need for security automatically justifies the attenuation of freedom, it becomes very easy for the security regime to be the norm, an everyday experience, and for freedom to fade like a vanished dream. The security measures must always be seen as proportional, temporary and exceptional departures from the norm of freedom, and the security agencies as fully and visibly accountable. As much freedom as possible must be preserved during the emergency. None of this is evident in the government's position and actions as stated above.

A further particular danger of the new surveillance and IT technology used by the security services is that it has the power to reverse the relationship between the state and the citizen, the social contract itself. As we shall see in chapter 10 on freedom and democracy, the essence of democracy, and what it shares with freedom, is that the government is accountable to the citizen and not the other way round. But the logic of universal surveillance is that the citizen is accountable to the executive arm of the state. Thus it is essential to freedom and democracy that the executive be, and be seen to be, *effectively* controlled by the other two arms of the state in the interests of individual freedom. The lines and the direction of accountability must be unambiguously clear, *especially* in emergencies. How far short present practice falls was explored in chapter 5.

It is also necessary to monitor continually whether the extra powers do result in the benefits claimed for them. It is not obvious that the benefits are always proportionate. In some respects, they may even be negative. Sir Tim Berners-Lee has asserted that the security services have, by breaking down encryption, made the internet a more dangerous place, not a safer one. Raab showed that the demand for 90 days detention without trial was not only grossly excessive but also unnecessary: all important arrests had been dealt with in 45 days.

Because of the need for secrecy, accountability is not straightforward. Select committees of the House of Commons cannot provide detailed oversight because MPs do not automatically receive security clearance. Indeed, when a committee is faced with security chiefs vehemently asserting that Edward Snowdon has disclosed some of their working methods with disastrous consequences, and then with the editor of *The Guardian* newspaper insisting that his disclosures include no such information, the very secrecy of the material prevents the committee from knowing the truth of the matter, or being able to decide between them. Thus the structure for safeguarding the freedom and privacy of the citizen depends on the judicature, and we have seen in chapter 5 that many of the functions and powers that properly belong in the courts have been taken over by the executive, breaching the separation of powers.

6.4 Emergency powers are not readily given up when no longer needed

A further threat can arise just as the emergency recedes and vigilance is relaxed. Emergency legislation, giving government sweeping powers, is not always repealed once the danger has passed. Such provisions can remain dormant on the statute book, to be resuscitated years later and used, for example, to protect a politician from embarrassment. In 1998 Lord Irvine of Lairg was appointed Lord Chancellor, and his official apartment at Westminster was refurbished in lavish style at a cost to the taxpayer of £650,000. Of this, £59,000 was for hand-printed wallpaper. For fear of public outrage, the contractors doing the work were compelled to sign the Official Secrets Act as if their work was a threat to national security.

Another of many examples occurred in the late 1970s, when the Callaghan government was approaching an election it was not confident of winning. An influential Cabinet think-tank researched the incidence and costs of heavy drinking, and concluded in its report that 'alcoholism' had reached the level of an epidemic; that the resulting costs were unacceptable; that all studies showed that the harms and costs were always directly proportional to the level of alcohol consumption per head across a population; that the only way to reduce the harms and costs was to reduce consumption; that the way to reduce consumption was to reduce availability; that the biggest factor in availability is price; and so the way to reduce consumption, harms and costs was to raise the price of alcohol. The Callaghan government saw this as a major vote loser, and suppressed the report under the Official Secrets Acts then in force, dating from 1911 and 1939, as if it was a threat to national security. It was then illegal to own a copy of the Cabinet report, and it could only be obtained under plain cover from abroad. This was so ludicrous that one academic appeared on television waving a copy at the camera, daring the authorities to arrest him. No one did.

That Cabinet report remains suppressed to this day, while successive governments flirt with the very powerful lobby of the drinks trade, and promote unconvincing token measures to curb public drinking when it makes the headlines. Consumption, harms and costs have continued to rise. According to Dr Foster's *Hospital Guide* of December 2013, 533,302 people had been admitted to hospital in the previous three years for symptoms directly related to the use of alcohol or illicit substances, alcohol being the prime cause in the great majority of cases. Alcohol-related crime, lost productivity and family breakdown have all increased. It is no coincidence that, according to a report in *The Sunday Times* of 29 June 2014 and a Channel 4 *Dispatches* programme, supermarkets are now selling lager more cheaply than mineral water, and a man can now drink his recommended daily alcohol limit for £1 and a woman for 75p.

(To be fair, there are real difficulties about raising the levels of excise duty and tax even higher than they already are. Such rises are indeed unpopular. The powerful lobby of the drinks and entertainment industries would resist any serious reduction in consumption. While the costs to the nation of dysfunctional drinking across all social budgets are enormous, the revenue from taxes and excise duty on the sale of alcohol is greater still, so the Exchequer has no interest in reducing consumption. And the tax rate in France is lower than in the UK, so that increasing the difference further would lead to an increase in smuggling. However, the health lobby would support such an increase.)

The point being made here is that the Cabinet report remains suppressed for political reasons under what was originally emergency legislation to protect national security. With this habit of retaining such legislation after the emergency has receded, contrast the attitude of Winston Churchill. As early in the war as 1943, he justified releasing Oswald Mosley, the leader of the English fascists, from detention in a telegram to the Home Secretary in these terms: 'Extraordinary powers assumed by the Executive with the consent of Parliament in emergencies should be yielded up when and as the emergency declines ... This is really the test of civilisation' (Cit. Raab, p. 51).

6.5 Freedom, security and politics

But the failure to repeal emergency legislation as soon as possible is only one danger. From the government statement quoted in section 6.1 above (pp. 100, 101), it appears that the law itself is being stretched in ways that Parliament has neither scrutinised nor sanctioned. It will take brave libertarian politicians to hold the government and the executive to account. When a nervous population wants protection above all else, those who advocate freedom are labelled and watched as subversives. Occasionally they can even be hysterically labelled as traitors, as if their vigilance for freedom somehow weakened security. We saw in chapter 3 how this is already happening. Anyone who has ever taken part in a demonstration is now logged on a police database as a 'potential extremist'. Free speech? A free country?

Our freedom will always depend on an informed, alert and vigorous public to ensure that limitations on freedom are scrutinised, challenged and minimised at every step, and that emergency powers are repealed at the earliest safe moment. This is especially necessary precisely at those times when security becomes an urgent issue, as now. Such citizens will constantly mandate their MPs to defend their freedom.

President Eisenhower was Supreme Commander of the Allied Forces in Europe during the Second World War, but, unlike some of his generals, he was no warmonger. It is worth recalling his warning in his farewell address to the nation when he stood down as President on 17 January 1961. He said:

> We must guard against the acquisition of unwarranted influence, whether sought or unsought, by the military-industrial complex. The potential for the disastrous rise of misplaced power exists, and will persist. We must never let the weight of this combination endanger our liberties or democratic processes. We should take nothing for granted. Only an alert and knowledgeable citizenry can compel the proper meshing of the huge industrial and military machinery of defense with our peaceful methods and goals so that security and liberty may prosper together. (Eisenhower's Farewell Address to the Nation. January 17, 1961)

He would now surely include the security apparatus.

Finally, Ken MacDonald, also making a valedictory speech on retiring in 2008 as Director of Public Prosecutions (cit. Raab, p. 119) said:

> We need to take very great care that we do not fall into a way of life in which freedom's back is broken by the relentless pressure of a security State ... very great care to imagine the world we are creating before we build it. We might end up living with something we can't bear.

114

7

Freedom and the Legislative Itch

*The best of all possible rulers is but a shadowy presence to his people,
for they say, it happened to us naturally.*
The *Tao te Ching*

*... for many years, nothing at all happened. It was a good system of
government, because most people want nothing to happen ... that is
the problem with governments nowadays. They want to do things all
the time. People want to be left alone to look after their cattle.*
Alexander McCall-Smith, *The Number One Ladies' Detective Agency*

We have seen that, in a country where the freedom of the
individual is a primary value, legislation is kept to a minimum.
By this standard, how should we rate ourselves?

Between May 1997 and August 2006, the 'New Labour'
government created an astonishing total of 3,023 new
offences. Of these, 1,169 were by primary legislation debated
in Parliament, and 1,854 by secondary legislation, under
powers delegated to other authorities, or by orders in council. Of 382 Acts of Parliament, there were 10 Health Acts, 12
Education Acts, and 29 Criminal Justice Acts. Between 1979
and 1992, Parliament passed 143 Acts concerning local government, of which 53 enacted structural changes. To give
some sense of scale, the administrations of Margaret Thatcher

and John Major had created 500 offences in their last nine years in office.

Further, the pace accelerated during the Blair years. During 1998, 160 new offences were created by primary legislation; during 2000, 346 offences were created; in 2005, no less than 527. This looks uncommonly like the rising need and dose of an addict.

Many of these laws were necessary and would enjoy public support, but many more showed what Nick Clegg called 'an obsession with controlling the minutiae of everyday life'. One makes it an offence to sell a grey squirrel or a ruddy duck. Some were ill-considered responses to single-issue pressure groups; others were passed for nakedly political ends.

Some were ostensibly good laws and yet show a disastrously wrong use of the legislative process. Consider, for example, the Road Vehicles (Construction and Use) (Amendment) (No. 4) Regulations 2003, which made it illegal to use a mobile phone while driving a motor vehicle on a public road. Nothing wrong with that, you might think. There is plenty of research to show that using a phone while driving distracts much attention away from the road. Texting while driving is obviously criminally lethal. But why just mobile phones? There are plenty of other distractions. Smoking while driving is at least as dangerous. So are trying to swat an insect, calming quarrelling children, conducting a fraught conversation, picking your nose ... where is the line to be drawn? The result is that the police are left to define as they please 'not being in control of the vehicle', thus becoming legislators and breaching the separation of powers.

Arguably, some modern cars are fitted with arrays of distractions, such as complicated ventilation systems, GPS screens, entertainment consoles and many others. Using law to try to control every detail of behaviour is futile. It also demonstrates a misunderstanding of the functions of law in a free country. One simple law creating an offence of being involved in an accident, reliably enforced and carrying serious criminal penalties, would concentrate the driver's mind on preventing accidents far more effectively than creating a mass of arbitrary, detailed offences. Further, like most good law, it would be largely self-enforcing.

The Labour administration had no monopoly of ill-considered legislation rushed through Parliament without sufficient scrutiny to placate single-issue pressure groups, although it did so in unprecedented amounts. The Dangerous Dogs Act 1992 was such an act, and it gave rise to many problems of interpretation and application. It had to be modified several times and is still being modified currently. Again, the attempt to regulate detail is self-defeating.

If laws are to protect and enlarge our freedom, they must be clear and enforceable as well as libertarian. We saw in chapter 1 the possibilities of bad law and its implications for the rule of law. The effective rule of law is essential to freedom, but Parliaments are not infallible. Laws that are muddled, poorly drafted or difficult to enforce are as much a threat to freedom as oppressive laws. Readers of Kafka are well aware of the terrifying unpredictability of incompetent government. Incompetence is not the only threat: legislators can also be manipulated and bought. Freedom does not mean laissez-faire government: quite the opposite. There can only be freedom where there is a government that is both efficient and libertarian. Edmund Burke observed that 'bad laws are the worst sort of tyranny'.

The responsible citizen, confronted by a law he considers bad, will obey the spirit rather than the letter of the law. The general attitude to the speed laws is a case in point. We will revisit this issue in a section of chapter 15 on victimless crime.

Politicians like to make laws because they want to be seen to be doing something, and that is what they do. Tony Blair, for example, had apparently read neither the *Tao te Ching* nor *The Number One Ladies' Detective Agency*. But we are a democracy, and our politicians represent us. It is not uncommon to hear people say 'There should be a law against it.' The legislative itch is not confined to politicians. But in a free country it should not be scratched too often.

> *Don't just do something: stand there.*
> Ronald Reagan

8

Freedom and Equality

.... our fathers brought forth on this continent, a new nation,
conceived in Liberty, and dedicated to the proposition that
all men are created equal.
Abraham Lincoln

The ideas of freedom and equality seem to belong together. If freedom is the default condition of human beings, then presumably all are equally free. John Locke mentions the two together (Second Treatise, 2.4), but without explaining the linkage.

The idea of equality he derives from Richard Hooker, an Anglican bishop and theologian of Elizabethan times, and one of the best minds of the English Reformation. Perhaps surprisingly, Hooker did not derive the idea of equality from his Christian beliefs. He did not state that all men are equal because God created us so, nor because Christ died for all equally. In what must have seemed a revolutionary way in those early post-feudal times, he adduced equality from the simple observation that, if I desire the respect of my neighbour, then I must show him the like respect. Our obligations to each other are mutual and equal, and therefore our rights must be equal also. This was clear, pragmatic and

119

independent of religious belief. Perhaps this was why John Locke would refer to him a century later as 'the judicious Hooker'.

The influence of Locke is apparent in the American Declaration of Independence, where the linkage is made explicit in the section quoted earlier in chapter 2, and in the French Declaration based on it. The French revolutionary motto of *Liberté, Egalité, Fraternité* makes it explicit also. It was the demand for both freedom and equality that was so subversive of the old order, and seemed so very threatening to the establishments of neighbouring states. This was especially true in the UK, where Thomas Paine, author of *The Rights of Man* and activist in both the American and the French Revolutions, was tried for treason in his absence and convicted. Other supporters of reform were also tried under hastily enacted laws, but juries refused to convict.

The linkage of the two ideas then fades. J.S. Mill does not make it in *On Liberty*. He makes it only in the context of marriage, in *The Subjection of Women*. In our own times, the reverse seems to be the case. Freedom and equality are now seen not only as separate, but as incompatible, even mutually exclusive. If capitalism is the economic expression of freedom, then under it some will become richer and others poorer, so, at least in economic terms, there is no equality. Equality can only be imposed by a command-and-control government, and then there is no freedom.

In Britain, the political right has traditionally stood for freedom and the left for equality, or at least for social justice, as the primary value. The British people are deeply suspicious of all dogma and extremes whether of the right or the left, preferring pragmatic to ideological parties and governments. In practice, government is always somewhere on the continuum between freedom and equality, well away from the extreme ends, and periodic elections give the country the opportunity to adjust that position to the left or to the right, increasing equality or freedom. (That is the theory. There are times when the parties are almost indistinguishable on this issue. Perhaps at those times the population is broadly content with its position on the continuum.)

In such a democracy, one of the limits on freedom will be the demands of the left for more social justice, such as the redistribution of wealth. That can only gain majority support if sufficient numbers of voters feel sufficiently poor, insecure or aggrieved to vote for social justice as against freedom. Further, if the gap between the rich and the poor is perceived as unacceptably wide, there exists a pre-revolutionary situation.

Freedom can then only be assured by rectifying the imbalance. It can only exist and flourish when most people are secure and content, when their primary needs have been met, and when the rich are not perceived as gross, exploitative or parasitic. Only then do the people have no reason to demand the imposition of equality by government. They will then place a primary value on freedom (if they vote at all).

Thus, by a circuitous route, we return to the link between freedom and equality. Absolute equality is impossible, but freedom in a democracy can only be assured if the population at large enjoys a certain level of dignity and security. Only then will people vote in numbers for freedom. The link is pragmatic, not theoretical.

9

Freedom, Law and Morality

Law may restrain bad behaviour;
it never made a bad man into a good man.
Anon.

They are always with us. Those who are utterly certain that they know what is right and wrong, not only for themselves but for everyone else; who are determined to impose their morality on everyone else by law, or by force if necessary: the puritan dictators, the enemies of freedom. The self-righteous, self-appointed guardians of other people's consciences, they appear in various guises, religious or secular. They tend to infiltrate and take over what were originally legitimate movements and take them to violent extremes, such as animal rights and pro-life organisations.

If one group or section in a country can impose on others its views on what is acceptable and what is unacceptable behaviour, clearly that country is to that extent not free. Therefore in a free country, law and morality will overlap but they do not coincide. Morality is then a matter of private judgement and choice, not law. Many behaviours may be regarded as unacceptable, and invite severe social disapproval, without being criminalised.

They may also give rise to a civil action for damages without being criminal. Examples of such civil wrongs, or 'torts', are libel and trespass. In such cases, the offence is seen as against an individual who can sue for damages, not as a criminal offence against society.

In countries that aspire to freedom, consensual sexual acts between adults, whether of the same sex or different sexes, fall into the category of private moral judgement so long as they satisfy Mill's principle and harm no one. Adultery is regarded in the same light, even though a betrayed or deserted spouse might be said to be harmed. Fidelity cannot be enforced by law without tyranny and a police state, and the attempt would change the nature of marriage as a voluntary commitment. It is essentially a civil matter between individuals.

The recreational use of illegal drugs provides another useful and challenging test issue. If Mill's harm principle were rigorously applied, it would involve disaggregating 'drugs' and assessing the harm caused by each substance separately. The harm caused by heroin or crack cocaine is not the same as that caused by cannabis or ecstasy. Only those drugs whose use was proved to risk harm to *others* would then be criminalised. In a free country, the onus of proof is always on those who would restrict freedom to show that the behaviour concerned at least risks harm to others, not on those who want that particular freedom to show that it does not.

On that basis, nicotine and alcohol, both addictive drugs that kill thousands, would be banned. The USA prohibited the sale of alcohol in the 1930s, with disastrous consequences including a large rise in violent crime. Prohibition had to be repealed and the drug decriminalised and restored to legitimacy. That these two addictive killer drugs remain legal is due to historical accident, not to any rational examination of the harm they do. Governments are dependent on the huge revenues they gain by taxing them heavily; tobacco

123

companies, distillers, brewers and vintners make huge profits from pushing their respective drugs, especially in developing countries, and wield enormous lobbying power which is not always publicly visible. For all these reasons, nicotine and alcohol sales and consumption will continue to rise across the world, regardless of the harm caused to people, families and communities.

But is that a reason to legalise drugs currently illegal? The users of such drugs who consider their habit to be harm-free may well feel aggrieved that drugs they regard as much more harmful than theirs continue to be legal, even socially encouraged, while their choice of substance puts them in danger of criminal prosecution. This clearly is unfair. But is that a reason to decriminalise some drugs – or even all drugs – currently proscribed? So far as the libertarian argument goes, clearly not. Harm is the only issue. Those who wish to criminalise the sale or use of a particular drug in a free country have to show that its use causes, or at least risks, harm to non-users, not that criminalisation (or decriminalisation) is necessary for fairness. Inevitably, evidence will be produced on both sides and hotly disputed. This is a healthy testing process for which freedom of speech is essential.

A clear example of law being used to impose on society at large the morality of a single-issue pressure group is the Hunting with Dogs Act 2004. This is an example of a vocal, puritanical lobby forcing its particular, passionately held morality on the rest of the country by law. It was successful due to the particular political circumstances of the time, and to that extent the UK is a less free country.

The instructive comparison here is with *sharia*. A Muslim state is a theocracy: Allah is the head of state and the only and absolute lawgiver. Therefore there is only one law, the *sharia*. What Allah forbids is both sin and crime: they are one and the same thing. Different Muslim states have historically interpreted this in different ways, some more tolerantly than others, but this view is not restricted to Islamists and jihadists. It is basic Koranic teaching. Many Muslims therefore find freedom a difficult concept. Some 'smell' its attractiveness, particularly those who have lived for any length of time in a relatively free country. Others, in very restrictive regimes, pick up the 'smell' of freedom through the web. Experience, personal or vicarious, can soften or illuminate a hard, legalistic interpretation.

The anti-hunting lobby confused morality with law in a similar way, assuming that law must enforce morality. Such thinking leads to the destruction of freedom. The ardent advocates of the Act followed it up with direct action in the field in the form of hunt sabotage. They were called 'the Taliban of the countryside'.

The only occasion when law will be used to enforce morality in a free country is when there is an overwhelmingly strong moral conviction that is held almost unanimously by the whole population. This used to be the case in the UK with regard to homosexual acts. That view is no longer sufficiently widely held to justify criminalisation. Examples still in force include laws forbidding dog-fighting, cock-fighting and bear-baiting. The first two are carried on in semi-secrecy in several parts of the country, but a proposal to legalise such practices on libertarian grounds would be unthinkable. In the case of the Hunting with Dogs Act 2004, the Countryside Alliance organised a mass rally of 40,000 people in London to demonstrate that the moral condemnation of hunting with dogs was by no means unanimous.

In a free country, law is used only to restrain behaviour that could harm someone, including such behaviour by the state. All other behaviours are matters of private choice. Such a society is morally pluralistic. For this to be realised, a general climate and practice of tolerance is essential. It is easier in times of plenty than in times of want or insecurity, and never easy where people with passionate and differing moral convictions live in close proximity and share common social institutions. The example of tolerance has to be set at the top of every sector of public life.

> *Tolerance is giving to every other human being every*
> *right that you claim for yourself.*
> Robert Green Ingersoll

10

Freedom and Democracy

If liberty and equality, as is thought by some, are chiefly to be found in democracy, they will be best attained when all persons alike share in government to the utmost.
Aristotle

What exactly is the relationship between freedom and democracy? They seem to be closely related, yet clearly they are different concepts.

The essential characteristic of democracy is that government is accountable to the people, and not the other way round. Thus both democracy and freedom are antithetical to top-down, authoritarian, hierarchical or centralised power. Both were, with equality, central to the demands of the revolutions of the modern era, from the English Civil War through the American, French, and European Revolutions. (Whether the new revolutionary governments always granted to the people the freedom, the democracy or the equality they had demanded is another matter.)

So are they necessary to each other? Logically, democracy should not be necessary for freedom. Theoretically, it should be possible for a ruler or a ruling clique to create and maintain a constitution designed to protect the freedom of the

citizens. But if the citizens only had the right of self-determination at the goodwill of the ruler, which could be withdrawn at any time, that would not be freedom in the
republican sense of freedom from domination, as we noted
earlier. To give real freedom, the ruler would have to give
away her own power completely and irrevocably. Lord
Acton's dictum, arising from a lifetime studying history, that
'All power tends to corrupt, and absolute power corrupts
absolutely' suggests that this is rare, because even those
acceding to power with the highest ideals are almost inevitably corrupted eventually by the compromises that are an
inescapable part of politics. Even if one is not so corrupted,
their successor probably will be.

It is not easy to find examples in history to disprove Acton.
The long list of revolutions seems to show that power is
never surrendered voluntarily; King John only signed Magna
Carta because he had no choice. But we may have one
exception in our own time: Nelson Mandela as president of
South Africa seems to have retained a consistent focus on the
freedom, democracy and equality of all the people of South
Africa without showing any signs of the corruption of power.
Perhaps he was the exception that proves the rule. His suc-
cessors have not consistently escaped tribal and other fac-
tional interests to put first the good of all equally.

In general, those in power are unwilling to share it, so to all
intents and purposes democracy is essential for freedom.
Democracy is the language of opposition; government seldom uses the word except when lecturing other countries on
the subject. Foreign secretaries may occasionally mention the
word; home secretaries never.

On the other hand, freedom clearly is a precondition of
democracy. There are many horrifying examples around the
world of what we might call show-piece elections, where
voters are intimidated, where no real alternative is offered,
and where the ballots are rigged. Clearly this is neither free

128

nor democratic. Democracy is more than elections. Only when all citizens have full freedom of speech, are able to debate and dissent without fear, are free to vote in secrecy and to establish their own political parties, and when the valid result is implemented, can real democracy function. As Sen puts it, 'basic civil rights and political freedoms are indispensable for the emergence of social values. Indeed, the freedom to participate in critical evaluation and in the process of value formation is among the most crucial freedoms of social existence.' (p.287)

Sometimes overlooked is another respect in which freedom is essential to democracy, and that is the free flow of information. Without freedom of speech and vigorous free media, not only are citizens ignorant and easily deceived, but government also may make disastrous decisions based on a mistaken view of facts, often grossly over-optimistic, fed to them by those seeking favours. In *Development as Freedom*, Sen describes how, during the Chinese famines of 1958–61, which killed nearly 30 million people, the authorities believed they had 100 million tons of food supplies more than they actually had. He quotes Chairman Mao himself as saying, in a speech just after the famine:

> Without democracy, you have no understanding of what is happening down below; the situation will be unclear; you will be unable to collect sufficient opinions from all sides; there can be no communications between top and bottom; top-level organs of leadership will depend on one-sided and incorrect material to decide issues ...(p. 182)

Indeed, Chairman Mao might have used the term *freedom of speech* as well as *democracy*.

There is at least a third way in which freedom is essential in a democracy. Even where a free and fair election has produced a democratically legitimate government, it is possible for that to develop into a tyranny of the majority, as we saw in chapter 1. Democracy alone provides no structural guarantee of toleration or freedom for minorities. Indeed, it can appear to sanction a tyranny by the majority. This is such a real danger that a constitutional safeguard for the freedom of minorities is essential. A possible form this might take is suggested in chapter 16 for incorporation in a modern Magna Carta.

Freedom, then, equally and justly distributed among *all* citizens, is a necessary condition for democracy. Where we wish to introduce or promote democracy, all efforts will fail unless the freedom of all citizens is first constitutionally and enforceably ensured.

There is a more basic reason for our intuition that freedom and democracy belong together. We saw in chapter 2 that a polity characterised by rights and entitlements leads logically and structurally to a passive and dependent population and a centralised and powerful state; and that, conversely, a polity based on the freedom of the individual citizen leads to empowered citizens and a government essentially accountable to the electorate. This inescapable structural reality shows that freedom and democracy share much of their DNA.

What are the prospects today for a democracy based in the freedom of the citizen? The omens do not look good. Voter turnout in the UK, even at general elections, has been disturbingly low and declining for years, inescapably showing a widespread scepticism, even cynicism, about the democratic process as now practised in the UK. Many years ago, Ken Livingstone wrote a book entitled *If Voting Changed Anything, They Would Have Abolished It* (Fontana Press 1988). I have no idea what was in the book, but the title struck a chord. (That was long before he was elected mayor of London: that voting was apparently acceptable.) The reality is that only voters in marginal constituencies can make a difference; other voters, the great majority, clearly think that they might as well stay at home. There are several other factors contributing to this alienation: sensational media coverage of scandals about MPs fraudulently claiming taxpayers' money as 'expenses', while honest MPs get neither coverage nor recognition; the dictatorial behaviour of party central offices towards local constituency activists, especially on selection lists; the bullying and bribing behaviour of whips, which has eliminated all independent thinking and free speech from the House of Commons; the puerile point-scoring that so often seems to pass for serious debate; the perceived conflicts of interest when MPs accept money from outside bodies; the perception that much power has passed away from Parliament to big business and to transnational organisations and corporations – these are just some of the factors feeding a widespread and dangerous disengagement from the democratic process. Together, they create a sense of powerlessness and futility. Such alienation provides fertile soil for the growth of subversive movements.

But from the moribund stump of the tree of democracy, a vigorous green shoot is appearing. Having been rather negative in chapter 2 about the web's effect on privacy, we can be much more positive about its effect on democracy. Online campaigning organisations such as 38 Degrees can make democracy work by enabling citizens to combine in supporting petitions on particular issues, addressed to MPs. These petitions can attract hundreds of thousands of signatures in a matter of days. They bring real pressure to bear on politicians on those issues which matter most to us.

Online democracy is superior to traditional voting in at least five ways. It is continuous (not once in five years); it is issue-based (it does not involve giving a blank cheque to a political party); it bears directly on the elected representative, making him accountable; its impact and the response are immediately visible; and it overcomes the numbers problem. It has long seemed that, while democracy might be very real in a small city state like ancient Athens, it can hardly be routinely meaningful in a population of many millions. Online democracy even turns large numbers to advantage.

The ease with which emails can be sent means that MPs receive large numbers of them. The number is a useful indicator of the extent of popular concern on each particular issue. Some complain of the extra work, even though they are provided with offices and allowances for secretarial help. If they complain of low turnout at elections, and then complain when large numbers of voters engage with the political process online, they cannot expect to be heard seriously. This large-scale engagement of voters reveals the true democrats: they welcome it as a relief from the apathy and cynicism expressed by low turnouts at elections. Those who decry it risk appearing as pseudo-democrats, especially if they further complain that some of the emails use the same form of words; that is no reason to discount voters' engagement.

Indeed, the effectiveness and impact of online democracy is shown by the ferociously negative reaction of some MPs. The shameful, bullying and abusive behaviour of the Business Select Committee towards David Babbs of 38 Degrees on 26 November 2014, on the subject of the Transatlantic Trade and Investment Partnership proposal (TTIP) shows with a chilling clarity the impulse to suppress democratic enquiry and dissent. There is a danger that the authoritarian, anti-democratic reaction could be institutionalised. An edited BBC report of the event can be heard on the 38 Degrees website.

There can be no doubt that online petitions are the one way to revitalise democracy. Rather than through electoral contests between political parties, this is how democracy now works. Ordinary citizens are free as never before to enjoy Sen's 'freedom to participate in critical evaluation and in the process of value formation [which] is among the most crucial freedoms of social existence'.

(Political parties appear to be in decline; they attract fewer and fewer members, donations from fewer but richer donors, and fewer and fewer votes. Some advocate propping them up with more public money, but the taxpayer has already been forced to pay huge sums to support zombie banks and zombie companies: why should she also be made to support zombie political parties? If they are not articulating voters' real concerns, they serve no useful purpose. Perhaps they should be allowed to wither, and make room for people of ability and integrity who want to serve their country to offer themselves for election as independents. Perhaps this way we might see the end of the 'last-night-of-term-in-the-prep-school-dormitory' style of debate, and at last see proper, grown-up statesmen debating serious issues with the gravitas they deserve. Perhaps even freedom of speech in the House of Commons!)

*　　*　　*

A paradox arises when a freely elected democratic government votes away its own freedom. This can happen when a government or a people is terrified by a threat, and either wishes to surrender to it or to give plenipotentiary power to a leader in the struggle for survival. At other times, freedom-with-responsibility can seem a terrible burden, as for the liberated Israelites who wanted to return to the familiar, comfortable security of slavery in Egypt (Exodus 16:2,3).

The same thing can happen on the individual level, when a person chooses servitude to gain security, or an addiction for relief or pleasure. Some mentally ill people choose to remain patients rather than face the responsibility that comes with freedom. Freedom can be traded away in a Faustian compact in return for another good, such as a security, perceived as more necessary or desirable than freedom.

It is in the nature of free choice that it will sometimes be used in a way that will bring unforeseen or undesirable consequences, both at the individual and democratic levels. Authoritarian, hierarchical anti-democratic powers have sometimes attempted to justify their power on the grounds that they know what is best for people better than they know themselves. The introduction of democracy has often been resisted precisely on these grounds. The case for freedom and democracy does not rest on any view of the wisdom of the electorate, but, as John Stuart Mill so thoroughly showed, on its necessity for human welfare and growth. Bad decisions are inevitable; but, as we saw earlier, they are even more likely in a dictatorship. They are the risk that has to be taken.

Elections belong to the people. It's their decision. If they decide to turn their back on the fire and burn their behinds, then they will just have to sit on their blisters.
Abraham Lincoln

11

Freedom and the Limits of Dissent

> *I disagree with what you say, but I will defend to the last
> your right to say it.*
> Evelyn Beatrice Hall, commonly but wrongly attributed to Voltaire

A government's attitude to dissent is the acid test of its libertarian credentials. A government that is anxious about dissent or satire betrays an authoritarian streak as well as a lack of confidence. A strong libertarian government, on the contrary, not only tolerates dissent but proactively encourages it.

The case for this view was argued powerfully by John Stuart Mill in *On Liberty*. An opinion or a policy can only be seen to be good if it is tested against alternatives, and can only be improved by such testing. It is entirely possible that policy options better than the government's may be offered by dissenters, and when this happens, a genuinely freedom-loving government will be glad to accept and acknowledge it. In a democracy, encouraging dissent and debate is also the best way to ensure that policy has the informed assent and ownership of a majority of the people.

Where can dissent be expressed? Sham 'consultations', where the general perception is that the decision has already been made, do far more harm than good. Where such

135

consultation is offered, people are put in a double bind. They must take part if they are to be heard and not dismissed for not taking part, but then suspect, rightly or wrongly, that they have merely provided plausibility for a bogus process. Suspect consultations promote a corrosive cynicism about democratic processes and about politicians and officials in general. Alienation is increased by the apparently excessive time and money consumed by such exercises.

As we saw in chapter 10, freedom of speech is essential to democracy. When investigative journalists are muzzled or fired rather than rewarded; when whistle-blowers lose their jobs instead of being rewarded; when employees lose promotion or their jobs for refusing to collude with deceit or illegality, or are silenced by blanket clauses in their contracts; when bank officials lose their jobs for warning their superiors of excessive debt; when inconvenient scientific research is suppressed; and when backbench MPs are prevented by bribes or threats from expressing an independent view, then to that extent we are looking at a country that is not free.

It does not matter what mechanism is used to suppress inconvenient dissent. It may be an abuse of an Official Secrets Act that has long since outlived its original cause; it may be an obscure and unaccountable administrative device; it may be an abuse of the libel laws; it may be by making the dissentient's life so unpleasant that she resigns of her own accord. The effect in each case is the same: dissent is suppressed, not welcomed, and with it freedom: not only the freedom of the person speaking, but also the freedom of everyone else to hear.

When a government or a management behaves in this way, it is clear that it has something to hide. Again, the purpose is as immaterial as the means. It may be to protect a politician or other powerful figure from disgrace or mere discomfort; it might be to prevent the hindering or discrediting of some planned project; it may be to enhance or depress the value of an asset such as a piece of land, or even a rigged interest rate or a currency. The effect is the same; and when such actions become the habitual style of a government or a management, while the suppressor may think he has got away with a particular instance, the effects accumulate over time to create a serious disaffection from all authority, and from what comes to be seen as a mockery of freedom and democracy. In a company, it destroys motivation and spreads a hidden alienation. Conversely, where a climate of alienation and cynicism develops, there is a prima facie presumption that management or government is responsible.

Government does have to maintain secrecy when the security of the state requires it, the issue discussed in chapter 6. Company managements have to maintain secrecy about technical, planning, financial and other matters. And there is the essential priority of privacy, such as of people's personal information, as discussed in chapter 3. The freedoms of information and speech do have to be limited by law in some situations in order to balance other interests, but none of that debars dissent.

Dissent is a principled challenge to a received or a proposed view or policy. Are there limits to dissent in a free country? For example, how is a free country to react to groups which, if they gained power, would destroy the very freedom that had allowed them to exist and to flourish? The alternatives are to proscribe them by law, or to allow them to exist and rely on a freedom-loving populace to contradict and contain them. The latter is to be preferred where possible, for all the reasons given above: the public debate will test the issues, heighten and sharpen public awareness and, above all, involve the population at large in responsibility for their own freedom and for their society.

Where legal proscription is necessary, it can have the opposite effect of depressing the people into passive dependence on government. But it has been found necessary where an organisation is inciting criminal acts or the subversion of the state. This is particularly threatening when such groups are being urged by a foreign power to commit acts of treason or other violence, and even more so when the foreign power is using religious ideals to motivate its adherents.

This was the case in the UK in the sixteenth and seventeenth centuries, when successive popes excommunicated British monarchs and encouraged such actions as Guy Fawkes's attempt to blow up Parliament. This put British Catholics in an agonising conflict of loyalties, between their British citizenship and their submission to Rome. A similar agonising conflict of loyalties is the experience of some British Muslims now, when respected imams or other authorities urge violent or illegal acts. One important difference is that the Catholics of the sixteenth and later centuries were British. Many young Muslims are British by birth, but have rejected British culture, and many Muslims have chosen to live in the UK. Another important difference is that Muslims are not bound to submit to a single absolute authority, and many strongly oppose the more extreme forms of jihadism.

The same issue arose with the fascists in the 1930s and with communists in the 1950s. Those groups and individuals that do promote illegality and the destruction of freedom (as by the forced imposition of *sharia*) have had to be proscribed in order to protect the rule of law. It is a false and dangerous kind of tolerance that allows such behaviours to go unpunished, and citizens have a right to have their freedom and safety protected by government. What else is government for?

The law, then, is there to protect freedom. When freedom under the rule of law is secure, dissent can be welcomed and encouraged as a useful contribution to public debate and policy formation. Only then can the British traditions of tolerance, and of hospitality to refugee immigrants, flower in the large walled garden of freedom.

12

Free Markets? Freedom and Money

> *Money is coined freedom.*
> Dostoevsky: *Memoirs from the House of the Dead*

Money gives choices. Those who have a lot of it have many options open to them; those with little have few. Therefore, at least in a cash economy, money is both essential and proportional to freedom.

If our proposed definition of a free country in chapter 4 is accepted, applying to every citizen, then a country can only call itself free if every citizen has at least enough money to meet basic needs, and a range of goods and services from which to choose the means. A freedom-loving country will aspire to more than the minimum for all its citizens in order to maximise freedom. Since our definition of a free country involves individual responsibility, excess income above the essential minimum should be dependent on contribution and proportional to it.

In the USA, the land of the free, the US Census Bureau stated in November 2012 that more than 16% of the population, nearly 50 million Americans, lived below the government's poverty line. How free are those people? In the UK, with the welfare state, there is application to all citizens of the basic minimum, at least in theory. Other countries have various mechanisms for distribution of wealth and the alleviation of poverty.

In a country whose prime value is freedom, all structures and institutions, including financial ones, are designed and maintained to maximise freedom for all citizens. How are financial and stock markets structured in a free country? There is a view, sometimes propounded as a dogma, that free, that is unregulated, markets are the economic expression of freedom. This view has always been the basic assumption in the USA, albeit sometimes modified by specific laws passed during financial crises, only to be repealed when better times returned. In the UK, there has been a shift towards this view since the deregulation of the 1980s.

Those who hold this view argue further that only unregulated markets generate enough wealth to provide the resources to ensure at least the minimum necessary for the freedom from want of all citizens.

How have such 'free' markets worked out? In the years to 2008, we witnessed an unsustainable bubble in asset prices caused by almost limitless cheap credit, recklessly distributed. Regulators and ratings agencies connived. Those in the banks and elsewhere who saw the inevitable crisis coming, and warned bankers and governments of excessive and unsustainable debt, were dismissed, in some cases literally, as party poopers. Banks, governments and markets rode the party to the terminus in what is now seen as a rush of reckless, irresponsible greed. 'Greed is good for the economy'? In 2008-9 it very nearly destroyed it. Banks were broken by rogue traders engaging in activities that their managers and directors did not really understand. But the money kept coming in, in huge amounts, so why ask questions?

The collapse of Lehmann Brothers nearly brought the entire global financial system down. Other banks were too big to fail and had to be bailed out by taxpayers on a scale that defies the imagination. To make matters worse, the very managers who had brought their banks and the economy to the brink of destruction were seen to be rewarded with more money than they could ever need, or even know how to use, while those on much lower pay who had worked for them were left in danger of losing their livelihoods.

Is this freedom? On Mill's definition and our proposed, updated version, it is only freedom if it does no harm, and insofar as it is governed by the rule of law. The 'free' markets did huge, nearly catastrophic, harm in 2008-9. For all the (costly and conniving) regulators and ratings agencies, it was not freedom, and these were not 'free' markets. This was pure anarchy.

What we see is regulators, authorities and commissions that seem to multiply in numbers as they decline in effectiveness. The taxpayer has to pay for these bodies as well as for the results of their failures. This causes harm at every level, to the taxpayer, to the investor, to the company and to the economy.

So what would banks, markets and other financial institutions look like in a truly free country? Intervention, by governments or central banks, such as ultra-low interest rates or 'quantitative easing' may be essential in a crisis, but often leads to unintended consequences such as distorted markets. It can be difficult to withdraw from such interventions once the crisis has passed, because markets and currencies have then become dependent on them.

In a free country, the role of government and central banks in markets should be minimal and arms-length, to provide and maintain self-balancing market structures within which the various stakeholders limit each other in the common interest, in a way analogous to the separation of powers in a national constitution.

In a company with such a structure, the element to provide

the necessary control on reckless and greedy managements is the shareholders, the owners of the business. One of the current imbalances arises from the hijacking by managers of control of companies from the shareholders. Shareholder resolutions on executive pay were not even binding on managements until 2013! Managers have then used this stolen control indirectly to pay themselves whatever they like; and they like a lot. This almost amounts to theft from the shareholders, and is therefore a legitimate point of intervention by the legislature.

The scandal is so great that EU regulators have limited bonuses, and the UK government has attempted partial reform. But these measures have proved ineffective: the banks have continued to pay the same amounts of money to their senior executives by increasing salaries and creating variable 'allowances' that look strikingly like bonuses. The HSBC had the effrontery to announce this in its annual report for 2013 while also warning that pay-outs to investors would be flat for the first nine months of the financial year.

Returning control, particularly control of remuneration and incentives, to the shareholders is not straightforward where a majority of the shares is held by large institutions such as pension funds. The chief executives of such funds and companies may serve on each other's remuneration committees, creating an indirect conflict of interest. At the least, they have an interest in maintaining or raising the general level of remuneration. At this they have been staggeringly successful: 'In fact, executive pay has become a kind of racket, with a small club of non-executives voting for huge pay rises for each other.' (Source: Matthew Lynn, *Money-Week*, 11/7/14).

One suggestion by Davide Serra, who is chief executive of Algebris, a British government adviser, is that if institutional investors do not at least publish how they voted at AGMs, they should not receive the dividend.

It is the private investor who has been deprived of effective control of the company she owns. It is a further irony that it has been government policy to attract citizens to invest their savings by offering tax breaks through PEPs, TESSAs, ISAs, SIPPs and other such schemes. Having wooed such investors, the government has a duty to them. This must include ensuring their control as owners. Perhaps private investors should form a majority on remuneration committees.

Companies would still have to compete internationally for the best talent, but a start might be made in changing the culture, reducing the general level of remuneration and ensuring that incentives do not skew objectives. In particular, private shareholders might be expected to have longer-term perspectives than managers, so that a move away from destructive short-termism might become easier, not only in incentives but across all policy issues. However, empowered shareholders are no more virtuous than individuals representing pension funds, so the structures, checks and balances must still be carefully constructed and maintained.

Only when management has been returned to proper accountability to the owners of the business will anything like a functional balance between interests be created, setting each free to achieve their maximum for the good of the whole, and reducing the need for regulation and political interference.

Mill's harm principle applies to markets and other financial activities just as it applies to all other sectors of individual and national life. Where harm is caused, it is the duty of the state to legislate to prevent it, limiting freedom as little as possible. Creating and maintaining a self-balancing structure should be the aim here as in the constitution.

*   *   *

This chapter has attempted to address the question of the balance between freedom and regulation, and the roles of governments and central banks, in financial markets and company governance. I have not ventured to approach the larger questions of those roles in economies, with questions such as whether unlimited cheap credit really gives freedom. These questions are vital and fundamental, but lie outside the scope of this book. There is a large and expanding literature on them already.

> *Give me control of a nation's money supply,*
> *and I care not who makes its laws.*
> Mayer Amschel Rothschild

13

Freedom and Religion: Are They Compatible?

However true (our opinion) may be, if it is not fully, frequently fearlessly discussed, it will be held as a dead dogma, not as a living truth.
John Stuart Mill: *On Liberty*

All states aspiring to freedom and influenced by rationalism have enacted constitutions that specifically prohibit any alliance between the state and any one religion. Freedom of thought and belief is sometimes specified in addition. The one exception is the UK, whose constitution is unwritten and which has a religion established by law, the Church of England. However, this has not precluded freedom for other religions. The axiomatic separation of religion and state can be seen as a reaction against the abuses of the religious monopoly of the papacy in the Middle Ages. Mill, quoted above, saw that pluralism, dissent, challenge and debate were essential not just to freedom but also to healthy belief.

Yet all is not as it seems. In some states that disallow a state religion, one religion – usually Roman Catholicism – has nevertheless established a position of overwhelming dominance, as in France, Spain, Italy, Ireland and much of Latin

145

America. In Ireland, the Church long had a virtually controlling influence over legislation on moral issues such as abor-
tion and birth control, and over education throughout the
country. It was even able to prevent the publication in
Ireland of the works of such authors as James Joyce, George
Bernard Shaw, Oscar Wilde and Samuel Beckett. The
church's enormous power was already waning before
the paedophile cover-up scandal dramatically weakened it
further, but until recently the Church's influence in Ireland
was much stronger, and wider in scope, than the influence of
the Church of England in English politics and social life.
Constitutional disestablishment does not guarantee religious
freedom or pluralism. There is much greater religious freedom and pluralism in the UK, with its established Church,
than in some of these nominally secular republics.

Another development that gives pause for thought is the
way in which some secular republics have replaced religious
rituals with state ones, such as saluting the flag, singing
patriotic songs or saluting images of The Leader. It is almost
as if some form of religion is necessary for social control and
cohesion, needed by governments so long as they control it.

What, then, is religion? There have been many books
written by theologians that have attempted to define religion
by its content. Is it about gods? But that would exclude
Theravada Buddhism, clearly a religion but not interested in
gods. Life after death? That would not accommodate Shinto,
and perhaps not Judaism. If we want a useful definition of
religion, we should ask not the theologians but the social
anthropologists. From living among and studying 'undeve-
loped' tribes, it becomes clear that the tribe's religion consists of its myths, which may or may not have a foundation in
historical fact but give the tribe its identity, and its rituals,
which are the mechanism by which the tribe transacts its
business across internal and external boundaries. An obvious
example is rites of passage.

146

The tribe's religion serves as a social glue, a vital bond ensuring tribal cohesion. The *lig* stem is the same as in *ligament*, and it is our ligaments that hold our joints and our body together. Religion can therefore also be used as a means of social control.

A further dimension is added by considering that such tribes, whether hunter-gatherer, fishing or farming, live close to nature, acutely aware of the massive forces which can destroy them at any time. One attempt to control these forces is to construct them as gods and then attempt to bribe them with sacrifices. Again, religion is a control mechanism. Whether it is successful or not is a different matter.

Social anthropologists, then, define religion not by its content but by its social function, as a facet of the tribe's corporate and social life. It is not a matter of personal beliefs. When members of the tribe are engaged in a ritual, their personal beliefs and doubts are not in play. Indeed, they may harbour serious doubts about the religion. That does not mean that they are being insincere or hypocritical in their religious observance.

The response of the individual, to the contrary, is defined as faith, and this may be independent, or even critical, of the tribe's religion. Prophets and protest figures are powerfully motivated individuals challenging an established religious hierarchy on grounds of personal faith and vision.

This view may suggest that rulers of all sorts will feel the need of a set of myths and rituals that they control. If they are to govern, they need to write the narrative. If a new set of beliefs begins to gain support that acknowledges a power higher than the ruler, it must be either suppressed or co-opted. Both things may happen, so that a state-sponsored and official version and an illegal, underground version of the same religion may exist in parallel in a totalitarian state such as soviet Russia or contemporary China. Their beliefs may be similar, but they will be suspicious of each other.

147

How does this play out in a free country? Religious pluralism means that the country is not a single tribe with a single
religion, but a collection of tribes each with its own myths
and rituals, with individuals being free to belong to the tribes
of their choice. Mass global movement and migration means
we are in an experimental stage, still working out how to
combine social cohesion with freedom, pluralism and
mobility.

The overall identity and cohesion of a tribe or a country
may be partly expressed through shared cultural experi-
ences, such as sport (essentially a tribal activity with its own
myths and rituals) and widely watched television programmes, causing moral issues to be worked out in public
spaces such as the workplace (last night's programme: will
he, won't he? Should she, shouldn't she?). This is likely to
diminish as scheduled viewing gives way to selected viewing
on the web. Other social institutions such as the NHS may
command widespread support and thus provide some
cohesion.

The most fundamental social glue other than religion is
common interest, so the shared economy is the area in which
fairness and openness are, or are not, worked out. This is
easier when there is no shortage of key commodities, such as
employment, education and housing, but more problematic
when shortage causes tribes to compete, and to scapegoat
each other. It is then that a desperate government may be
glad of a common enemy or threat, the most effective social
glue of all. We noted in chapter 6 that such threats may be
exaggerated, or even invented, to create cohesion in times
when a government may be at risk.

Even in a country with no national religion, there are still
social functions that need some form of religious observance.
Moments of great significance in people's lives need to be
marked by some ritual. Birth, marriage and death are the
obvious examples: these are not purely private events. They

require some social expression and recognition, a ritual by definition.

Perhaps we are ritual-starved. Would it be helpful to have rituals to mark divorce, or the beginning and ending of a working life? Some bodies such as The British Humanist Association are creating non-religious rituals. Is that an oxymoron?

Similarly, there are state occasions when the country as a whole needs to express a shared emotion on a significant matter. Remembrance Day is just such an occasion, as are royal weddings and funerals. Consciously religion-free ceremonies to mark such occasions seem to lack the resonance provided by religious reference to realities, values and aspirations beyond the immediate present, and common to all.

Religion, then, can be regarded as a (possibly pathological) substitute for faith at the individual level, but as a necessity and a benefit at a social or national level. In a truly free country, people are free to form and practise their own choice of religion, subject to Mill's harm principle and the rule of law. The state may offer but not impose a form of religion to meet personal and social needs, but it cannot use religion as an instrument of social control and must protect citizens from religious bodies that would do so.

To try to regulate the internal affairs of a family, the relations of love and friendship, or many other things of the same sort, by law or by the coercion of public opinion, is like trying to pull an eyelash out of a man's eye with a pair of tongs. They may pull out the eye, but they will never get hold of the eyelash.
Sir James Stephen: *Liberty, Equality, Fraternity*

14

Freedom, Literacy and Development

Thank God there are no free schools or printing; ... for learning has brought disobedience and heresy into the world, and printing has divulged them ... God keep us from both.
Sir William Berkeley, Governor of Virginia, d. 1677

The liberating power of literacy and education has long been known, and feared by entrenched authorities. Before the Civil War in the USA, there were severe penalties for anyone who taught a slave to read. This is also the reason for the Taliban's murderous opposition to women's education. Once people can read, they might get ideas ...

This is not necessarily or always true of education. Schooling can be used to indoctrinate, and has been used in this way in totalitarian states. Perhaps it always does indoctrinate, unavoidably. Literacy, however, truly liberates, not only because the reader has access to worlds of ideas denied to the non-reader, but also because it greatly increases the person's chances of gaining employment or other means of making a living, bringing self-sufficiency with all the dignity and morale-boosting energy that follow. Illiteracy and poverty are connected; so literacy is linked to sufficiency, capability and freedom.

The literate person is also able to navigate official bureaucracy; and not only to navigate it, but to assert her rights against oppressive administration, and to form a critique of it. Voting, too, becomes much more practicable, and so democracy becomes more widespread, better informed and more intelligent. After food and health, literacy is the great liberator.

Literacy also opens the door to education. In the ferment of the 1960s and 1970s, there were many books advocating various degrees and kinds of revolution in education, most of them wanting to use schools to change society, such as *Deschooling Society* by Ivan Illich (Penguin Books, 1971) and *Teaching as a Subversive Activity* by Neil Postman and Charles Weingartner (Penguin Books, 1969). They were typically intellectualisations of the diffuse but vigorous anti-establishment temper of the times. Some of them applied to the USA rather than to the UK; almost all have sunk without trace. The work of just one of those writers has survived to develop a thoroughly worked-out theory and praxis of education and literacy as instruments of freedom, that of the philosopher Paolo Freire. In the 1960s he was active in Brazil, his home country, and Chile, his country of exile. He remained active until his death in 1997. His analysis derived from Franz Fanon and Karl Marx among others, but nevertheless led to the subversion of any tyranny. His books, particularly *Education as the Practice of Freedom* (Writers'and Readers' Publishing Co-operative, 1976) and *Pedagogy of the Oppressed* (Penguin Books, 1996) have become standard texts in education courses in the USA and around the world. UNESCO awarded him its Prize for Education in Peace in 1986 and his ideas inform several UNESCO projects.

The flavour of his thought can be gained from this excerpt from *Pedagogy of the Oppressed*:

Education either functions as an instrument which is used to facilitate integration of the younger generation

151

into the logic of the present system and bring about conformity or it becomes the practice of freedom, the means by which men and women deal critically and creatively with reality and discover how to participate in the transformation of their world.

His best-known term is *conscientisation*. He rejected what he called the banking model of education, where the pupil is seen as like an empty bank account into which the teacher pays credits, in favour of a collaborative model in which the pupil is actively engaged. For example, when children in a slum school learn to spell the word *slum*, discussion will explore what a slum is, and why some people have to live there and others do not. Until such conscientisation occurs, people do not even know they are poor. They do not have a name to put on their condition, and can see no way out of it or that there are alternatives. 'Conscientising' people to their condition opens the way out of it, setting them free.

Literacy is where education and freedom begin. But they need a context in which to take effect, and this context is usually called development. This is still sometimes seen as something done to 'developing' countries by 'developed' countries. This generally takes the form of 'aid' which consists of cash transfers and the secondment of skilled professionals from the former to the latter. Development outcomes are often measured and evaluated in economic terms, such as by growth in gross domestic product or of income per capita in the 'developing' country.

One professional economist has exposed the limitations of such assumptions and metrics. Amartya Sen, who won the Nobel Prize in Economic Science in 1998, holds that freedom is the only true way to achieve *and* measure development. In his book *Development as Freedom* (Oxford University Press, 1999, p 4) he sets out his thesis thus:

152

Freedom is central to the process of development for two distinct reasons:

1 the evaluative reason: assessment of progress has to be done primarily in terms of whether the freedoms that people have are enhanced;
2 the effectiveness reason: achievement of development is thoroughly dependent on the free agency of people.

Sen sees freedom as *capabilities*: 'A person's "capability" refers to the alternative combinations of functionings that are feasible for her to achieve. Capability is thus a kind of freedom ...' Sen's *capabilities* are very like the *choices* suggested in chapter 4 as part of a definition of a free country, but with one significant difference. In my Introduction to this work, I excluded from its scope physical freedoms, or abilities. The focus was to be solely on legal or social freedom, sometimes called *normative* freedom because it has to do with the norms, legal or customary, of a society. Sen's *capabilities* include physical as well as normative freedom. In the context of development, it makes no sense to focus on either physical *or* normative freedom exclusively. If a person is too weakened by hunger or disease to attend meetings or to travel to a polling station, what use is civil freedom or democracy? Sen instances countries where people are normatively free but physically unfree, and other countries where the reverse is the case. His thesis is that development can only be accomplished, and can only be measured, by the total capabilities of the people receiving aid. These will include freedom from hunger, from avoidable disease and mortality, and from illiteracy, as well as civic, social and political freedoms such as participating in the democratic process. These are both the means and the measure of development. Money is obviously a prime essential for these capabilities, and enough money to make a real difference. But in Sen's analysis financial aid is instrumental rather than constitutive of development as freedom. Money is a means, a necessary means, but not a sufficient end in itself. If people have the capability of earning their own living, that is better than passive dependence on aid.

Sen does not reference Freire, but their vision is the same. If Freire sees freedom as the goal of literacy and education, Sen sees it as the goal and means of development. Across the philosophy-economics frontier, they share Mill's vision of freedom as an essential condition for humanity.

One of the implications of Sen's view is that, if development is to be seen and measured in terms of freedom, development and freedom are matters of degree, never perfectly achieved, constantly ebbing and flowing in both 'developed' and 'developing' countries. We have seen that freedom is under threat, and being seriously eroded, in 'developed' countries, so 'development' is needed here too. Similarly, in 'developing' countries, serious efforts are often made at the point of delivery to involve recipients actively in decisions on the use of aid. The distinction between active 'developed' and passive 'developing' countries is largely invalid and unhelpful. A model of shared values and enterprise would best serve the interests of both.

But it is not easy to break down us-and-them assumptions which are still widespread, especially among taxpayers in donor countries. Perhaps we should invite people from 'developing' countries to come and teach us to value our freedom, and its equal and universal distribution, while we still have some.

15

Further Issues

This chapter merely indicates further freedom-related issues. Each demands a book on its own; to address them here would make this work dauntingly large. The issue of freedom affects virtually every part of our lives, certainly all the parts that matter most to us. The less is written, the more is read, so these are mere pointers.

15.1 Freedom and the victimless crime

There are crimes that appear to harm no one. This is sometimes pleaded as justification for actions that are clearly indefensible. There are people who would not steal from a person but who do steal from an entity conceived as impersonal, because 'they will not miss my little bit'. Such a person might not steal from a corner shop managed by its owners who are known local figures, but would have no compunction over pilfering or shoplifting in a supermarket, or 'fiddling' their expenses, an insurance claim or their tax return. These actions do cause harm by raising costs and therefore prices for everyone else.

Yet there are indeed actions that are forbidden by law but

which harm no one. One common example of such purely 'technical' offences is breaking the speed limit when it is perfectly safe to do so, satisfying Mill's harm principle by risking no more harm to others than if the speed was slightly lower and legal. Conviction for this harm-free 'crime' can nevertheless lead to serious consequences: three convictions for such offences within three years will lead to disqualification and forfeiture of one's driving licence. This is a huge loss of freedom in itself. It also leads to large financial penalties in addition to the fine: when the disqualification expires and the person seeks insurance, the premiums will be much higher because of the disqualification. Loss of one's driving licence for three purely technical offences, without any allegation of dangerous driving, is seen by many otherwise law-abiding drivers as clearly excessive punishment. Disqualification is logically and morally equivalent only to dangerous driving.

When the law creates a genuinely victimless crime, it clearly violates Mill's basic assertion quoted in chapter 1 above: '... the only purpose for which power can be rightfully exercised over any member of a civilised community, against his will, is to prevent harm to others'. In such a case, it is not the 'offender' who is at fault, nor the enforcing agency, but the law itself. The speed limit laws are clearly, and always have been, bad law. They assume that, on a given stretch of road, there is one safe maximum speed for all drivers, in all kinds of vehicles and in all conditions, which bears no relation to reality. For this reason, otherwise law-abiding drivers, especially those with experience and skill, have always sought to evade law enforcement, while driving safely. The speed limit has thus always been difficult to enforce, which is an indication that the law does not command the respect of many drivers, *especially* the most skilful. From the earliest days of the motor car, this attitude was so widespread and general that the AA (Automobile Association) was founded to put scouts on the road to warn otherwise law-abiding drivers of police speed traps.

The speed limits are bad law for other reasons also. They isolate speed from other factors in road safety, such as visibility, road surface and traffic density, when, in reality, the safe speed is always relative to these and other factors. They also focus some of the driver's attention on watching for law enforcement, such as speed cameras and mobile patrols: attention which good law would focus solely on safety. The improvements in enforcement technology have in some ways made matters worse. If the letter of bad law is efficiently and zealously enforced, the results can be very unjust.

We have seen above that the rule of law is essential to freedom, but, since legislators are human, there are bad laws. The law-abiding citizen obeys the purpose and the spirit of such laws, which is both more demanding and safer than adherence merely to the letter of them, and seeks their reform.

15.2 Freedom, diversity and the European Union

EU standards are generally voluntary; and industrial standards can be very useful to all concerned, including customers. But in some matters, particularly 'harmonisation', the Commission is widely perceived as having an agenda of standardisation across the whole of Europe, so that aligning the practices and even the cultures of member states becomes an end in itself. One notorious example is Commission Regulation (EC) No. 2257/94, which stipulates a required size and curvature for bananas, which are not even grown in Europe. This is still in force, but has been subjected to such ridicule that, so far as I am aware, it is not enforced.

Vine growers in France and Italy who wish to use no chemicals at all, the natural wine movement, find themselves under severe pressure to conform. This is not the same as organic wine production, which allows up to 40 chemical additives, or biodynamic production. In April 2014, Emmanuel Giboulot, a grower in Burgundy, was fined €500 for refusing to spray his grapes with a particular pesticide. He could have faced a six-month imprisonment and a fine of €30,000: an online petition in his favour with half a million signatures may have mitigated the sentence. The interests of chemical companies coincide in this case with the harmonisation agenda. Similarly, Stefano Bellotti, a farmer in Piedmont, planted peach trees among his vines, which he believes is an ancient way to protect them. The EU authority ruled that his land could no longer be defined as a vineyard and withdrew €30,000 in subsidies. (Source: *The Sunday Times*, 13/4/14).

Such attempts at 'harmonisation' are bound to repel all citizens who value the particular culture and freedom of their own country. Both the French and the Danish have at different times voted against further harmonisation, at least partly for these reasons. It seems a counterproductive strategy for drawing European states together.

In the UK, there is a widespread perception that the nation's freedom is once again being threatened from the European mainland, although this time not by military means. Regardless of how much validity there might be in this view, it has political consequences. Among these is a risk that a decision on British membership of the EU will be made on emotional rather than rational grounds, and on the wrong issues.

For the purposes of this work, the issue raised is when standardisation or 'harmonisation' destroys freedom. Clearly, it destroys freedom when it destroys diversity, which is both a condition and a result of freedom. It is a condition of freedom because, in terms of our proposed definition in chapter 4, if there are few or no options available, there are few or no choices to be made and therefore little or no freedom. It is a result of freedom because, as we saw in the Introduction, freedom in the sciences and the arts, and in innovation and trade, leads to the florid diversity that is essential to social health and development.

Even in the natural realm, where biodiversity is both essential to the health of gene pools and a sign of such health, human activity has a tendency, whether intended or not, to reduce diversity, with potentially damaging consequences. The impulse to uniformity is one result of the lust for control, the antithesis of freedom.

Are there any circumstances where standardisation does not threaten freedom? Industrial standards can be beneficial when they eliminate choices that are not beneficial. Having two formats for video recorders, VHS and Betamax, did not afford freedom: buyers had to bet on which would prevail. Because one would inevitably fail, it was not a real choice but a gamble. Diversity, like freedom, is intrinsically valuable but not an unqualified absolute good. It is not good when it does not offer choice. We have four different formats of light bulb in our kitchen alone, but that does not offer choice: it merely imposes on us the necessity to hold stocks of all those formats.

The test of standardisation, then, whether from the EU or elsewhere, is whether it promotes or reduces the number of *useful* choices. Who decides which choices are useful? This is one of the areas in which democratic process is essential. One of the doubts many have about the EU is its perceived democratic deficit. Thus 'harmonisation' can be widely experienced as alien and imposed, the antithesis of freedom and diversity.

15.3 Freedom and 'health and safety gone mad'

When people are told that they cannot perform some ordinary action, perhaps one they have performed routinely and harmlessly for years, because it would be 'contrary to health and safety legislation', they are understandably frustrated and angry. They are apt to mutter about 'health and safety gone mad', about 'the nanny state' robbing them of responsibility, and perhaps about 'little Hitlers' and no longer living in a free country.

Typically, the people invoking this alleged legislation are not officials of the Health and Safety Executive, but managers of such premises as care homes, schools, clubs or activity centres, whether owned by councils or commercial bodies. Examples abound. In a north Somerset care home, residents were not allowed to hang pictures on their walls or have ornaments on their tables because they might fall off: it was 'health and safety'. Yo-yos in playgrounds, conker contests, knives in kitchens and kettles in offices have all been banned on this pretext. A pub customer was told he could not carry a tray of drinks from the bar to his table, a charity shop refused to sell knitting needles and an airline passenger was told to stop sucking a boiled sweet – all on grounds of 'health and safety'. For more examples see the *International Business Times* for 1 April 2014.

The appropriate government minister, Mike Penning, intervened. He showed that, in many cases, there is no basis in legislation for such prohibitions. Managers sometimes use the formula as a cover-all phrase useful for controlling people's behaviour. In some cases it is to cover sheer laziness – a room without pictures or ornaments is more quickly dusted than one with them – and in some cases out of a not unreasonable fear of being sued if anything goes wrong. The Health and Safety Executive is understandably unhappy about being blamed for such behaviour and has set up an independent 'Myth Busters Challenge Panel' to dispel such misperceptions. Anyone prevented from performing an action on grounds of 'health and safety' can refer their case to the panel, which will adjudicate. The panel has made some trenchant comments on what it sees as misuse of the term in particular cases.

So when does health and safety legislation unjustifiably reduce the freedom of the individual? The definition of freedom proposed in chapter 4 regards responsibility as a part of freedom. If this is accepted, then any law or action that reduces a person's responsibility reduces their freedom. In a free country, that has to be justified as necessary to prevent harm to at least one other person. A recent example is regulations limiting the kinds of electrical work a householder may do in his own house. There is risk that incompetent work by a householder may create a fire hazard not only to his own family and home but to those of neighbours as well. But how remote is that risk? To justify such limitation of what a person may do on his own property, there would have to be persuasive statistics of fires so caused, just as road safety measures are not taken without proof of risk. In practice that means statistically significant records of actual harm.

There have long been many laws on the statute book that protect us from ourselves. It is arguable that laws requiring drivers to use seat belts or motorcyclists to wear helmets do just that. They do not satisfy Mill's principle of preventing harm to others, and show the state taking some responsibility away from the individual: the 'nanny state'. Can such laws be reconciled with the idea of a free country? If so, where is the line to be drawn? Are dangerous games like rugby football or sports like skiing to be banned, or allowed only with specified protective clothing? Games and sports are not essential to our lives in the way that travel is.

It would now be unthinkable to repeal the laws requiring seat belts and helmets. They have become embedded in the lives of people and in the culture, accepted as limiting freedom and responsibility for the sake of the greater good of saving lives. But we should note that laws to protect us from ourselves are in principle antithetical to responsibility and freedom, and oppose laws proposed in the future that relieve people of responsibility.

15.4 Freedom in crowded communities

This is merely to observe one unavoidable reduction in freedom. When people live in scattered homesteads, their lives impinge little on those of their neighbours. They can manage their land or put up buildings as they choose, and make as much noise as they like. They are also responsible for meeting their own needs.

When we live together in settlements, these freedoms are necessarily reduced to balance with those of close neighbours. The greater the density of population, the more freedom has to be abridged. When houses are close and gardens are small, bonfires can only be lit in very specific weather conditions and at certain times of day. Often they will not be possible at all. In some places there are bylaws forbidding them. Trees such as *cupressus* will have to be kept within a certain size. When people live still closer to each other, as in blocks of apartments or flats, there will be strict limits on noise such as loud music, and on behaviour in shared spaces.

With more and more people living in cities, many unemployed and poor, freedom becomes increasingly limited. Many studies have shown that overcrowding causes violent conflict among rats, and similarly among people. Freedom is just as important to the human spirit in crowded cities as anywhere else, perhaps more so. The just distribution of space and freedom, with the resources necessary to secure them, is not only morally imperative: it is also politically wise.

16

A Modern Magna Carta

As noted in the Introduction to this work, the risk for 2015 is that the 800th anniversary of Magna Carta will be marked by a series of showpiece events without the legal force of the original. On the one hand, it would be seen as an instrument to use with such people as Muslim students in British schools, and on the other as a means of getting past the occasion without having to consider the real threats to the freedom of citizens today or more robust limits on executive power.

The key difference is legal enforceability. Magna Carta 1.0, with habeas corpus and trial by jury, has formed the basis of the courts' defence of the freedom of the individual for 800 years. If Magna Carta 2.0 does not restore and strengthen the traditional constitutional checks and balances, and address new threats, in enforceable ways, then it is a cynical confidence trick on the British people. To return to the Introduction, count the abstract nouns and noun phrases, such as liberty, equality, democracy, tolerance, access to justice, the rule of law, no one above the law – these are not enforceable, and are therefore a smokescreen. If we miss the opportunity to strengthen liberty, it is further threatened. To relate in any meaningful way to Magna Carta 1.0, it must be specific, concrete and enforceable at law against authority. The hope must be that the Commons Select Committee on Political and Constitutional Reform will propose a process that could lead to such a result.

Any real modern Magna Carta would surely include as a minimum:

- the social contract, with the state's only essential function being to protect the citizen's freedom from all threats, internal and external, and the citizen's commitment to knowing and using the language, to observing and upholding the law of the land; and to defending the country when required;
- the strict separation of powers, with robust checks and balances for ensuring the supervision of the executive by the judiciary, and its accountability to Parliament;
- the independence of the judiciary;
- the democratic accountability of the government to the people, not the reverse;
- the role of the monarchy as embodying the values of the nation;
- the restoration of habeas corpus to all process unless specifically excluded by Parliament, and the recognition and entrenchment of judicial review;
- the right to trial by jury for all indictable offences;
- specified classes of cases that may be heard in closed court with clear accountability;
- effective and visible democratic supervision of the security services and the police;
- free media licensed to investigate all use of power but liable in civil law for intrusion not necessary to the public interest, as defined;
- the right to privacy, subject to the public interest as defined;
- the encouragement and limits of dissent;

- provision for the abridgement of freedom and democracy in times of national peril, with limits and accountability specified;
- provision for amendments to the charter.

All the above merely restore and strengthen British tradition and best practice. Much has changed and much has been learned in 800 years, and both processes are accelerating. There should therefore be some new provisions. One new candidate for inclusion might be a Constitutional Court, or a power of the Supreme Court, with all members able to sit sitting, to strike down, with a specified majority, any legislation seen as unnecessarily infringing rather than protecting the freedom of the individual citizen; and any infringement of the separation of powers. This is admittedly controversial. It might be argued that, without a written constitution, all such judgements by the Supreme Court would necessarily be subjective. This is true. Yet in the USA with its written constitution such judgements are delivered by judges appointed by a party politician who is head of the executive, as we saw in chapter 5. A written constitution is no guarantee of judicial neutrality. Our own judges can be better trusted to be wholly party-neutral and strictly professional so long as their independence is enshrined in law and secure.

It might also be argued that it is not democratic to give judges power to strike down the acts of an elected Parliament. But it would be democratic if the court's power was conferred, defined and limited by Parliament. Also, without a written constitution, there is no way of binding future Parliaments, so the sovereignty of Parliament is automatically assured. There is no difference in this respect between a modern Magna Carta and the existing human rights legislation.

Such a power would be one available safeguard against an 'elective dictatorship' of the majority, which, as we observed

165

in chapter 10, is essential if freedom for minorities is to be safeguarded. We also saw in chapter 2 that no less an authority than Sir Edward Coke in effect affirmed just such a power.

Ideally, a truly modern Magna Carta would also attempt to define the rights of internet users so far as possible within the jurisdiction. The principle could be consistent with that established in the Acts and Settlements that followed the Civil War at the end of the seventeenth century, namely government and taxation only with the consent of the citizen. This might translate as using the user's private information, whether stored on paper or on digital media, only with the informed consent of the user. This would protect the user from unwarranted and unchosen government surveillance, press intrusion, commercial exploitation and criminal activity.

What could be the agenda of anyone resisting any of these proposals?

This is a charter, not a constitution, even though it borrows heavily from the American model. Writing a full and detailed constitution would be a much bigger undertaking lasting many years, and give opportunity to those so inclined to drag it out indefinitely. Even if we think a written constitution is desirable (and the American model is so far not proving robust against a security apparatus out of control), we should not wait for that.

What practical differences would flow from a modern Magna Carta? After all, the entitlements of the welfare state are not going to be abrogated, and such rights will continue to play a very important part in people's lives. However, it is encouraging to note a tendency even in the Labour Party towards recognising the responsibility principle by relating more benefits to contributions. Beyond that, further increasing the democratic accountability of the police should improve the level of trust and co-operation between police and public. Similarly, restoration of habeas corpus to general use unless specifically excluded would go some way to restoring the priority of freedom. Establishing a right to privacy of the person, of premises and of communications, balanced with the requirements of security and free speech when in the public interest, should give much more certainty and confidence than at present, especially to journalists. Restoring judicial processes to the courts from the Home Office, local authorities and tribunals, would assure people of due process.

The burden of proof should always lie with those who would erode the citizen's freedom and privacy. Tackling these difficult issues in the context of a *genuine* modern Magna Carta would help to keep freedom, and the state's responsibility for protecting it, in the forefront of people's awareness as an absolute value and priority.

King John only signed Magna Carta because he was compelled to do so. Governments since have only acknowledged their people's freedom as a result of revolutions. We are a democracy: we must demand a real Magna Carta 2.0.